PLANTS OF COLONIAL DAYS

Raymond L. Taylor

ILLUSTRATED BY
Dorothy L. Park

DOVER PUBLICATIONS, INC.
Mineola, New York

Published in Canada by General Publishing Company, Ltd., 30 Lesmill Road, Don Mills, Toronto, Ontario.

Published in the United Kingdom by Constable and Company, Ltd., 3 The Lanchesters, 162–164 Fulham Palace Road, London W6 9ER.

Bibliographical Note

This Dover edition, first published in 1996, is an unabridged republication of the second printing, 1959, of the work originally printed by The Dietz Press for Colonial Williamsburg, Incorporated, Williamsburg, Va., in 1952. The original subtitle, *A Guide to One Hundred & Sixty Flowers, Shrubs, and Trees in the Gardens of Colonial Williamsburg*, has been omitted in the present edition. In the original edition the illustrations were printed in a separate color.

Library of Congress Cataloging-in-Publication Data

Taylor, Raymond L. (Raymond Leech), 1901–
    Plants of colonial days / Raymond L. Taylor ; illustrated by Dorothy L. Park.
      p.   cm.
    Originally published: Williamsburg [Va.] : Printed for Colonial Williamsburg, 1952 (1959 printing).
    Includes bibliographical references and index.
    ISBN 0-486-29404-8 (pbk.)
    1. Plants, Ornamental—Virginia—Williamsburg. I. Title.
SB407.T35   1996
635.9′09755′72509033—dc20
                                 96-27687
                                      CIP

Manufactured in the United States of America
Dover Publications, Inc., 31 East 2nd Street, Mineola, N.Y. 11501

INTRODUCTION

This small book is particularly intended for any visitor to the gardens of Colonial Williamsburg who may wish to identify the plants there or to learn something more about them; it is also hoped that it will be of interest to gardeners everywhere whose pleasure in old favorites is enhanced by some knowledge of their history.

Just as naturally as the colonists brought with them to America their household belongings, their kitchen utensils, their tools and books, so, many of them packed away in their baggage seeds, bulbs, and even cuttings of their favorite plants. It is to be expected that fruit trees and kitchen-garden produce would have been thought of at the outset, but ornamentals were not forgotten, and before long they, too, were growing side by side with native plants brought into cultivation in colonial gardens. If we accept the testimony of John Josselyn, who first visited America in 1638, many European flowers were mingled with native species from the very beginning of the colonial period.

The architecture of the restored buildings of Williamsburg, and their interior appurtenances, are as completely authentic as expert research can make them. The landscape architects have been equally faithful in their task of re-creating the gardens of the eighteenth century. The basic work of investigation involved in restoration is difficult at best, and, once authentic species are known, further patient and critical appraisal is required for the selection of truly old horticultural varieties. Plants are living things, responsive to their environment and to the care they receive, so that individuals of the same species may appear confusingly different under diverse conditions. The problem is further complicated since nearly all garden plants have been selected, crossed, and "improved" since colonial times. Certain plants used ornamentally have been hybridized, either naturally or artificially, for centuries—or even for thousands of years, as in the case of chrysanthemums. On the other hand, with most native species growing wild, variations from the form and color known to the colonists are relatively slight, so that here one can be reasonably sure that these are essentially the same as two or three hundred years ago. Surviving drawings or detailed descriptions establish some garden forms without doubt, but with others it is not possible to be absolutely certain that the present generations of "old-fashioned" plants are identical with those of colonial days. Finally, when a correct variety is known, there still remains the problem of obtaining it today.

But the difficulties of the search for authenticity, though formidable, should not be overemphasized. Although it is true that one cannot transport back into a colonial garden a botanist or a horticulturalist trained in the modern sense, and it is also unfortunately true that very few actual herbarium specimens of the period remain, yet much can be accomplished even though it becomes necessary to fall back upon references to plants *by their names.* Written records of this sort are available; there is, in fact, a considerable body of documents, manuscripts, and books, some with colored plates as well as descriptions, that afford the necessary information on the plants in the bygone gardens of America. Though garden catalogues were not generally issued in America before the nineteenth century—with two notable exceptions in those of John Bartram and William Prince—such lists did exist in the British Isles. In addition, there are letters, orders for plants, invoices, garden notebooks, diaries, and advertisements, all of which provide fundamental data. In interpreting all such source material, a proper caution, of course, must be exercised with respect to the exactitude of plant names.

Botany as an avocation long antedates its present professional status, and it was not unusual for proprietors of colonial gardens to use Latin names gleaned from their perusal of ponderous botanical dictionaries and herbals written in Latin; but scientific names, in the now accepted binomial form of genus and species, date back only to 1753, when the first edition of *Species Plantarum,* by Linnaeus, appeared. Pre-Linnaean terminology is difficult for the uninitiated, but it is possible for the botanist with a historical bent to trace the identity of the more distinctive species back through the herbals of Parkinson, Gerard, and others, to such very early writers as Pliny the Younger, Dioscorides, and Theophrastus. In each period, however, references must always be carefully weighed and some basic assumptions made.

Scientific names, as now established, have obvious advantages: they show relationships, since closely related species are grouped together in one genus; frequently they tell—to those who know their Latin and Greek—interesting facts about the geographical origin of plants, their medicinal uses, or the like. Above all, a scientific name is *exact,* it never refers to more than one particular species, and it is internationally understood.

In contrast, common names vary inevitably with language from country to country, from region to region within a country, and from century to century. The same common name may be applied to more than one plant—as witness the regrettable confusion about the various "laurels" and "myrtles," which actually belong to different families. And the same plant may have many common names; the little flower known picturesquely as Quaker lady, bluet, innocence, and forget-me-not is only identified with certainty as *Houstonia caerulea.* When exactitude is important, the case must be conceded to the botanists.

Common names, nevertheless, cannot and should not be abandoned. It would be absurd for a gardener to resort to *Viola tricolor hortensis* when pansy would convey his meaning just as certainly. Moreover, common names often have meanings intrinsically interesting or of historical importance because they reflect some aspect of the culture of the times. In the days of the herbalists, who were the botanists of the fifteenth, sixteenth, and seventeenth centuries, it was customary to add to the descriptions and woodcut pictures a list of the "vertues" attributed to each plant. It was then widely believed that all the ills to which the flesh is heir could be cured or alleviated if the proper plants, or "simples," were used in the approved manner. A long list of names, such as "healall," "liverwort," and "heartsease," for example, perpetuates this ancient lore and, incidentally, tells us of the many pains suffered by our forebears, and their hopes for comfort and relief. According to the "Doctrine of Signatures," widely held among the herbalists, most plants indicated the use for which they were ordained by some sign, perhaps the shape or texture of the leaf or some detail of the flower.

Many plant names have come down to us with their meanings obscured, but they nevertheless afford pleasure for their fanciful or poetic charm, and they offer a challenge to those who are intrigued by words and their origins. For all these reasons, we have chosen to arrange the plants in this book in alphabetical order by their common names—but the scientific names have been added for final identification. It will be noted that this arrangement separates plants that are very closely related botanically, for example, African marigold and French marigold, or loblolly pine and white pine. A purely botanical manual would group such plants together, by genera and by families, but this has seemed unnecessary here. If the reader will consult the Index he will also find "Marigolds — African, and French," and such other groups as daylilies, hollies, oaks, roses, et al., with their separate page references.

A word must be said on which plants have been included and which omitted. The plants considered are restricted to one hundred and sixty of those trees, shrubs, and garden flowers that are the *principal* species used as *ornamentals* in the restored gardens of Williamsburg. Eliminated are the cultivated fruits; plants for the kitchen or herb garden, so numerous they might fill a book by themselves; and those "difficult" groups, the grasses, rushes, and sedges. Also ignored are the too familiar, too successful, ubiquitous forms called "weeds." Lastly, one will look in vain for such well-known plants as forsythia, common yellow jasmine, and Chinese wisteria; all these were introduced into North America after the eighteenth century, and therefore are not planted in the gardens of Colonial Williamsburg.

This book, also, is concerned only with plants that are known to have been used, or can reasonably be assumed to have been used, by the Virginia colonists. They fall into several categories: 1) local native plants with showy flowers or other attractive qualities, such as redbud, Carolina allspice, Carolina jessamine, dogwood, and the beautiful stewartia; 2) native plants from further south, for example, silver-bell tree; 3) native plants with some special usefulness—the thorny Osage orange for cattle-confining hedges, or Oswego tea for its supposed medicinal qualities; 4) European plants, familiar, desirable, and imported for the same characteristics for which they were cherished in the home country—box for ornamental hedges, or colorful tulips for mass effects; and 5) exotics from other continents imported into England and thence to America (or in a few cases introduced directly)—for example, such early curiosities as the paper mulberry from Japan, the ailanthus from the Moluccas, and the "African" marigold from Mexico.

4

Much research remains to be done on the history and authenticity of ornamental plants in the American colonies, for there are sources yet to be explored. Since the first planting of the gardens at Williamsburg, species have been added in the light of new information, and a few corrections have been made. Following the excellent pioneer accomplishments, the work of re-creating the gardens of another day goes on.

In the following pages, the names of certain early plantsmen occur again and again. These are the collectors, the travelers and explorers, the gardeners on both sides of the Atlantic, to whom we are indebted in such large part for our knowledge of eighteenth-century plant material. To assist the reader further, a few biographical notes on these important personalities are included here, together with references to the more readily available editions of some of their books, diaries, and letters.

Reverend John BANISTER (1650-1692). A Church of England missionary and a naturalist, with a plantation near Petersburg, Virginia; his list of plants drawn up in 1680 was published in Ray's *Historia Plantarum*. A fall, incurred while collecting, resulted in his death, thus terminating a promising series of scientific contributions.

John BARTRAM (1699-1777). By inheritance a Pennsylvania farmer, John Bartram became, in the words of Linnaeus, "the greatest natural botanist in the world." On horseback, by boat, and on foot, he ranged repeatedly into the forests from Canada to Florida and into the Ohio Valley. He visited Clayton, Custis, Garden, and other botanists, and had scores of correspondents on both sides of the Atlantic, notable among them Peter Collinson, who sent him European plants, and arranged for Bartram to supply American plant material to a number of English patrons. Bartram's garden, at the confluence of the Schuylkill and the Delaware, was the country's first strictly botanical garden. His paper, entitled in part *Observations on the Inhabitants, Climate, Soil, Rivers, Animals, and other Matters Worthy of Notice,* was first published in Philadelphia in 1751. *Diary of a Journey through the Carolinas, Georgia and Florida, from July 1, 1765, to April 10, 1766,* has been annotated by Francis Harper (American Philosophical Society, Philadelphia, 1942).

William BARTRAM (1739-1823). Poet, naturalist, and artist; the son of John Bartram. The vivid descriptions of nature in his travel books exercised a profound influence on the work of Coleridge and Wordsworth. *The Travels in Georgia and Florida, 1773-74,* has been annotated by Francis Harper (American Philosophical Society, 1943).

William BYRD II (1674-1744). A wealthy planter of Virginia. Like his father, Colonel William Byrd, from whom he inherited the plantation Westover, he served as a member, and later president, of the Governor's Council. His library was one of the finest of his time in America. He recorded his observations on natural history as well as life in colonial Virginia. *William Byrd's Natural History of Virginia* is available in a translation by Richard Croom Beatty and William J. Mulloy from a German edition (Dietz Press, Richmond, 1940).

Mark CATESBY (*c.* 1679-1749). An English naturalist, whose interest in America was enhanced by the marriage of his sister to Dr. William Cocke, of Williamsburg. Catesby lived in the southeastern states from 1712 to 1719 and returned later for another three or four years. The first volume of his *Natural History of Carolina, Florida and the Bahama Islands,* beautifully illustrated in color, was issued in 1731, and the second in 1743. It is an outstanding source book of native plants and contains a number of first descriptions of American species.

John CLAYTON (1685-1773). An English naturalist who came to Virginia in 1705 and held—for fifty-one years—the post of Clerk of Gloucester County. His garden at Windsor, in what is now Mathews County, greatly impressed John Bartram. His *Flora Virginica,* published by Gronovius at Leyden (1743), and his correspondence with other botanists, gave him a well-deserved reputation abroad. The spring beauty, *Claytonia virginica,* was named for him. The Arnold Arboretum has reproduced the 1762 edition of *Flora Virginica* (Boston, 1946).

Cadwallader COLDEN (1688-1776). A Scotsman well trained in botany who emigrated to Philadelphia in 1710 and later moved to New York State to become first Surveyor General and then

Lieutenant Governor. As an avocation, he engaged in the study of history, medicine, and botany, and corresponded widely with those of like interests.

Peter COLLINSON (1694-1768). A wealthy English Quaker woolen merchant, friend of Benjamin Franklin, whom he encouraged and helped in his work on electricity. He maintained an extensive correspondence with American naturalists, especially John Bartram. His famous garden at Mill Hill contained many American plants; conversely, Bartram's garden in Philadelphia profited from European plants sent by Collinson. The genus *Collinsonia* commemorates him.

John CUSTIS (1678-1749). A prominent citizen of Williamsburg, whose garden prompted John Bartram to comment to Collinson that it was second only to Clayton's. His correspondence with Collinson, available in *Brothers of the Spade,* by E. G. Swem (American Antiquarian Society, Worcester, Mass., 1949), depicts both the joys and trials experienced by early gardeners in their exchange of plants across the Atlantic. George Washington, through his marriage to the widow of Custis' son, came into possession of a part of the Custis property and was administrator for the share of his stepchildren.

John ELLIS (1710-1776). An Irishman engaged in commerce who traveled to Florida and the West Indies. His American correspondents, notably Dr. Garden, furnished him with material on both the flora and fauna of the colonies. He is credited with the first demonstration of the animal nature of corals and he suggested the generic names *Halesia* and *Gardenia* to Linnaeus.

John FOTHERGILL (1712-1780). After Collinson's death, this Quaker physician was John Bartram's principal correspondent in London. He financed William Bartram's Florida trip.

Alexander GARDEN (1728-1791). An Edinburgh-trained physician of Charleston, South Carolina, who came from Scotland as a young man. He was an active collector of plants and corresponded with Linnaeus, Ellis, and other botanists. Cape jasmine, or gardenia, *Gardenia jasminoides,* is a permanent memorial to him.

Thomas JEFFERSON (1743-1826). One of the most versatile men this nation has ever produced, a scientist diverted into statesmanship. His *Notes on the State of Virginia* and his *Garden Book* are excellent sources on ornamental plants in the colonial period. The latter has been edited and annotated by Edwin Morris Betts in *Thomas Jefferson's Garden Book 1766-1824, with Relevant Extracts from his other Writings* (American Philosophical Society, 1944).

John JOSSELYN (?-1675). An Englishman who lived in New England in 1638, 1639, and again from 1663 to 1671; he wrote several books on the animals and plants of the region, including *New England Rarities Discovered, 1672.*

Peter (or Per) KALM (1716-1779). A Finnish pupil of Linnaeus who was sent to America in 1748-49 by the Swedish Royal Academy to study plants, and explored from Philadelphia to Montreal, 1748-51. His acute observations, in diary form, were published in Sweden and in an English translation in 1770. This has been edited by Adolph B. Benson, *America in 1750: Peter Kalm's Travels in North America* (New York, Wilson Erickson, Inc., 1937). The genus *Kalmia* was named for Peter Kalm.

Carolus LINNAEUS (Carl von Linné) (1707-1778). The great Swedish botanist, professor at Upsala University, who placed the *naming* of plants and animals on their present basis of binomial nomenclature, which eliminates long, cumbersome individual descriptions and emphasizes plant or animal relationships within genera. The first edition of his *Species Plantarum* appeared in 1753. Linnaeus received American material from Garden, Colden, John Bartram, Mitchell, Clayton, Ellis, and from his pupils, including Peter Kalm.

André MICHAUX (1746-1802). A well-traveled French botanist who spent ten years collecting from Hudson Bay to Florida, sometimes accompanied by his son François André (1770-1855). In 1801 his great work on American oaks was published, but his *Flora Boreali-Americana* appeared posthumously.

John MITCHELL (?-1768). A practicing physician and justice of the peace in Urbanna, Virginia; he was probably born in the British Isles, whither he returned to end his days. His correspondents included Linnaeus, Bartram, and his first professor of botany at Edinburgh, Charles Alston. His map of eastern North America,

8

used in negotiating peace at the end of the Revolution, is still referred to; his technique for treating yellow fever saved many lives in Philadelphia's epidemic of 1793. The partridgeberry, *Mitchella repens,* was named for him by Linnaeus.

John David SCHOEPF (1752-1800). A Hessian surgeon and author who, in 1783-84, traveled from New York to Florida and the Bahamas, accompanied on the southern part of his journey by two Austrian botanists; his *Travels in the Confederation* is full of interesting comments. A translation by Alfred J. Morrison was published by W. J. Campbell, Philadelphia, 1911.

Lady SKIPWITH (?-1826). Jean, wife of Sir Peyton Skipwith, was an enthusiastic gardener at their home, Prestwould, on the Dan River, Virginia. Her *Garden Notes of 1793,* revealing many plants grown in colonial gardens, have been published by the Garden Club of Virginia in *Garden Gossip,* X, 1935, Nos. 2, 4, and 6.

Thomas WALTER (*c.* 1740-1789). A native of England who, as a young man, settled on the Santee River, South Carolina. Material for his *Flora Caroliniana* (London, 1788), listing more than a thousand plants and remarkably complete, was collected within an area of twenty-five square miles.

George WASHINGTON (1732-1799). Whenever his services to his country or to his community permitted, Washington took pleasure in developing the agricultural possibilities of Mount Vernon and in beautifying the grounds. All through his diary there are frequent references to the plants he cultivated. This valuable source of information is made available in *Extracts and Memoranda from George Washington's Diary Relating to Trees and Plants* (Houghton Mifflin, 1925).

In addition to the works already named, the following contemporary sources cannot be omitted from even so brief a summary: John Lawson's *A New Voyage to Carolina,* London, 1709 (reprinted as *A History of North Carolina,* Garrett and Massie, Richmond, 1937); Philip Miller's *Gardener's Dictionary,* London, 1711; and Richard Bradley's *Dictionarium, Botanicum,* London, 1728. In the next century, Sir Joseph Paxton collected a wealth of information, especially on introduction, in *A Pocket Botanical Dictionary,* London, 1840.

The two large, handsome volumes of *Gardens of Colony and State,* compiled and edited by Alice G. B. Lockwood (Scribner's, 1931, 1934), contain much interesting material on the early gardens of America. *The History of Horticulture in America to 1860,* by U. P. Hedrick (Oxford, 1950), covers a somewhat wider field. For those who wish to know more about the botanical aspects of the plants in this book, L. H. Bailey's *The Standard Cyclopedia of Horticulture* (Macmillan), available in most public libraries, is recommended. The one-volume *Taylor's Encyclopedia of Gardening* edited by Norman Taylor (Houghton Mifflin, 1948) is comprehensive and excellent.

ACKNOWLEDGMENTS

In gathering material for some years for a reference book on the history of ornamental plants in colonial America, and in preparing this handbook, I have been helped greatly by many persons—not all of whom can possibly be named herein. I am particularly indebted to the late M. L. Fernald, Director, Gray Herbarium, Harvard University; the late Alfred Rehder, Associate Professor of Dendrology, Arnold Arboretum, Harvard University; Conway Zirkle, Professor of Botany, University of Pennsylvania; Francis W. Pennell, Curator of Plants, Academy of Natural Sciences of Philadelphia; and W. C. Muenscher, Professor of Botany, Cornell University, for their assistance with books, herbarium specimens, or advice; to Earl G. Swem, Emeritus Librarian, and Miss Margaret Galphin, Assistant Librarian, College of William and Mary; to Mrs. G. Glenwood Clark, formerly with Colonial Williamsburg, who provided personal notes; to Mrs. Viola Gompf Evans, a former student; to J. B. Brouwers, Landscape Superintendent Emeritus, Alden Hopkins, Resident Landscape Architect, and all other staff members of Colonial Williamsburg, past and present, concerned with this publication; to Edwin M. Betts, Professor of Biology, University of Virginia, and Norman Taylor, Editor, *Taylor's Encyclopedia of Gardening,* who read this book in proof but are not responsible for any errors; and finally to my wife, Francena M. Taylor, whose abiding interest in plants and whose personal assistance both prompted this effort and led to its conclusion.

African marigold—*Tagetes erecta*

African marigold is a misnomer, for the plant is a native of Mexico, whence it was introduced into England in 1596. Marigold is a corruption of Mary's gold, and is applied to various yellow flowers in bloom at the time of the festivals of the Virgin. The genus may be named for Tages, an Etruscan deity; the specific name is Latin for "upright," not a particularly distinguishing characteristic in this case. The large, clear yellow or orange flower heads, with few to many, more or less crinkled "petals" appear on plants about 2 feet high, in summer through fall. The leaves are much divided or dissected—and strongly scented. John Gerard grew this marigold in his London garden. It was mentioned in Lawson's *History of Carolina,* and advertised for sale in Boston in 1760. Thomas Jefferson "sowed . . . Marygold," on April 2, 1767. Probably this was *Tagetes,* which belongs to the sneezeweed tribe of the Compositae. (See also French marigold.)

Ailanthus—*Ailanthus altissima*

The ailanthus is also called the tree of heaven, a translation of *ailanto,* the name given to a closely related species by the natives of the Molucca Islands in reference to the great height these trees attain. The specific name means "highest." Other common names are Chinese sumac and stink tree, referring to the unpleasant odor

of the staminate flowers. The large compound leaves have eleven to forty-one narrow, tapering leaflets, arranged like the parts of a feather. The fruits (on pistillate trees) appear in dense clusters of yellowish-brown, papery wings, each containing an imbedded seed. In 1751, seeds from Nanking, China, sent by Father d'Incarville, a Jesuit missionary, were received by Peter Collinson in England and probably reached the American colonies soon afterwards. There is an anecdote that some of the Virginia colonists believed the strong peanutlike odor of staminate trees repelled mosquitoes. The ailanthus is a member of the quassia family, Simarubaceae.

Althaea—*Hibiscus syriacus*

The althaea, or rose of Sharon, a shrubby member of the mallow family, Malvaceae, blooms in July and August. By their shape and many stamens, the rather large pink, flesh-colored, purple, or white flowers clearly show relationship to the hollyhock and the tropical hibiscus. The leaves, coarsely toothed and more or less triangular, are distinctive, as are the fruits, 5-valved woody capsules that remain throughout the winter. Originally from China and India, the althaea was introduced into England in 1596 by way of Syria, which accounts for the specific name, *syriacus*. *Hibiscus* is the Latin name for a mallow. Thomas Jefferson "planted . . . seeds of Althaea" on April 4, 1767, listing it as a shrub "not exceeding 10 feet in height." The althaea is mentioned in Washington's diary and Lady Skipwith grew "double white, & common Althaea" in her garden at Prestwould. (See also hollyhock.)

American beech—*Fagus grandifolia*

The American beech is a native species with a wide natural range that extends from New Brunswick to Florida, and westward to

Minnesota and Texas. *Fagus* is Latin for "beech"; *grandifolia* means "large leaves." Both the name "beech" and the word "book" are derived from the Anglo-Saxon *bēce, bōc,* because crude books were inscribed on thin boards of the wood. The smooth, light gray bark of older trees, the very long, sharply pointed buds, and the coarsely toothed leaves with numerous branch veins which leave the midrib at uniform intervals, are all characteristic. On young beeches, the leaves often persist until spring, a fact noted by Peter Kalm, who also wrote that, in Albany, gunsmiths burned beech for charcoal and the people of Montreal ate the nuts. In colonial times the wood was used for furniture, tool handles, and other woodenware. The American beech was introduced into England in 1766, as "Fagus ferruginea," and beech seeds were among the 105 species sent by John Bartram to his English patrons. The beech belongs to the beech family, Fagaceae.

American linden—*Tilia americana*

Lindens are known by many names, among them lime tree (formerly line, a variant of lind or linden), basswood, (*i.e.,* "bast-wood," in reference to the fibrous cortex of the bark), and white-wood. Linden is the Anglo-Saxon name for such trees. (Linnaeus derived his name from the linden since his father, when he became a churchman, had adopted the name Linné from an old tree in his garden.) *Tilia* was the Latin name for the European species; the Latinized adjective, *americana,* is geographically descriptive of this species, a native of the eastern United States. The American linden closely resembles other species here and abroad. Characteristic are the asymmetrical, heart-shaped, and coarsely toothed leaves; the bee-thronged clusters of small, yellowish-white, fragrant flowers that appear in June, hanging from green finger-shaped bracts; and, later, the small pealike nuts. The Iroquois made rope from the bark. Both John and William Bartram commented on the lindens seen in their southern travels. Peter Kalm referred to an "American lime-tree," and noted that mistletoe commonly grew on it. Thomas Jefferson in his *Notes on the State of Virginia* listed "Linden, or lime. Tilia Americana," as an ornamental and Washington planted it at Mount Vernon. All lindens belong to their own family, Tiliaceae.

American wisteria—*Wisteria frutescens*

The American wisteria, unlike the much more common Chinese wisteria (not known in the colonial period), blooms mid-May to

mid-June, *after* the leaves have appeared. The compact, drooping flower clusters, 2-4 inches long, are quite distinctive. The individual purplish flowers resemble the sweet pea, a member of the same great family of legumes, Leguminosae. The compound leaves are divided into seventeen to nineteen elongate-oval leaflets. Wisteria was named after Dr. Caspar Wistar (1761-1818), a Philadelphia physician and professor of anatomy at the University of Pennsylvania, by Nuttall, who chose to spell it wisteria—a version that, by rules of nomenclature, must persist. The specific name, *frutescens,* refers to the bushy shape the vine assumes if unsupported. This native plant, with a natural range from Virginia southward to Florida and westward to Texas, was introduced into cultivation in England in 1724. Thomas Walter in South Carolina, John Bartram in Pennsylvania, and Lady Skipwith in Virginia, all grew it in their colonial gardens.

Autumn crocus—*Colchicum autumnale*

English names for the autumn crocus, known in Europe a thousand years before Christ, are numerous and include meadow saffron and Michaelmas crocus. Theophrastus and Dioscorides knew of the potent drug, colchicine, contained in the bulbs; recently biologists have discovered that this alkaloid profoundly affects normal cell division. Linnaeus regarded Colchis, the ancient kingdom where the Golden Fleece of Greek mythology was kept, as the plant's country of origin and named the genus accordingly. Although the lavender, tubular flower of the autumn crocus, which blooms in August and September, resembles that of a true fall crocus, it actually is not even in the same family. True crocuses have but three stamens; the autumn crocus has six stamens and belongs to the lily family, Liliaceae. The first record of its appearance in America is 1760 when it was advertised for sale in Boston. Lady Skipwith included "Autumnal Crocus" among the "Bulbous Roots to get when in my power."

14

Bee balm—*Monarda didyma*

Bee balm or red balm is also called Oswego tea, because the settlers of Oswego, New York, learned this use from the Indians. Linnaeus named the genus in honor of Nicolas Monardes, physician and botanist of Seville, Spain; *didyma* means "paired," and refers to the two anther-bearing stamens that project beyond the flower. Blooming June through August, the bright red tubular flowers come from a large globe-shaped head. The plant is a tall mint with a four-angled stem and opposite leaves, fragrant when crushed — all typical of the family, Labiatae. Peter Kalm, in Philadelphia, October, 1748, wrote of the rivalry between humming birds for "the Monarda with crimson flowers." John Bartram collected the plant in Oswego, New York, for Peter Collinson, who grew it in his garden in 1744, although one record gives its first introduction into England as 1752. John Mitchell requested it from Bartram and, in 1757, John Hill wrote: "The modern Gardener is very well acquainted with the Plant, whose Fragrance and Colour demand a Place for it in every Collection and have made it nearly universal."

Bell-flowered squill—*Scilla hispanica*

This squill, known also as scilla, Spanish jacinth, Spanish bluebell, and wood hyacinth, flowers in April and May in a one-sided cluster of from five to fifteen blue, purple-blue, white, or pink bell-shaped flowers. The perianth segments are scarcely fused at the base but flared and curled; the leaves are about an inch wide. The word "squill," through the French *squille,* the Latin *squilla,* the Greek *scilla*—all names for this genus — comes from the Greek verb *skyllo,* "I injure," and refers to the poisonous nature of the bulbs of some species, notably the drug-squill, now *Urginea maritima. Hispanica* is from Hispania, Latin for Spain, the country of origin, whence the squill was introduced into England in 1683. White and pink varieties "from South Europe" were introduced there in the same year. Peter Collinson wrote John Bartram in 1737 "I shall endeavour to supply the Squills. . . ." The squill belongs to the lily family, Liliaceae.

Black-eyed Susan—*Rudbeckia hirta*

The black-eyed Susan, coneflower, or yellow daisy, is easily recognized by its long, yellow to orange "petals" and its dark brown, markedly conical central disk. The leaves are broadly lance shaped with toothed margins. The genus was named for Professors Rudbeck, father and son, who preceded Linnaeus at Upsala University in Sweden; *hirta* means "hairy" and refers to the short, stiff hairs on the stem. Blooming from June through August, it is equally attractive in hayfield or garden. This species, native to eastern North America, was first sent to England in 1714. A member of the sunflower tribe of the family Compositae, the black-eyed Susan is related to the coreopsis, also grown in Williamsburg gardens.

Blue iris—*Iris pallida*

The familiar blue iris of old gardens is one of the group of so-called "German irises." *I. pallida,* distinguished by its color, tall stout stems, and broad, swordlike leaves, is one of the parents of thousands of modern hybrids and other horticultural varieties. The genus was named for the Greek rainbow goddess, Iris, in reference to the prismatic colors of many irises; *pallida* means "pale"—this variety is light lavender-blue. The flower has three drooping outer perianth

segments and three erect inner ones, all with a "claw." *I. pallida* was brought to England from Turkey in 1596; an "Iris germanica" had been imported from Germany in 1573. John Josselyn mentioned "Blew Flower-de-Luce" and Captain William Byrd had iris in

Virginia in 1684. Both Jefferson and Lady Skipwith mention them and by the end of the eighteenth century there were frequent references to "purple flags" and the "Common Blue" in American garden notes. All irises belong to the family Iridaceae.

Blue monarda—*Monarda fistulosa*

The blue monarda or wild bergamot is native to the eastern United States; like bee balm, its close relative, it makes an excellent garden plant. The common name and the genus both honor the Spanish physician and botanist, Nicolas Monardes, author of *Joyfull newes out of the newe founde worlde,* first published in 1569. The specific name, which means "hollow" or "reedlike," alludes to the stem. The numerous tubular flowers that come from a large, globular head and bloom in June and July, are pale lilac or purple in color. This tall plant has the four-angled stem and opposite leaves of the mint family, Labiatae, to which it belongs. Choctaw Indians used its extract in an ointment for chest pains in their children. The plant was first introduced into England in 1656. Clayton mentioned the "Monarda with blue flowers" in his *Flora Virginica,* and Walter included it in his *Flora Caroliniana.*

Blue phlox—*Phlox divaricata*

This plant, native to eastern North America, is also called wild blue phlox or wild sweet William (although the last applies better to *P. maculata*). *Phlox,* Greek for "flame," applied originally to

red-flowered plants of the genus *Lychnis* in the pink family, and was transferred; *divaricata,* which means "spread out," refers to the plant's growth habit. The pale lilac-blue or white tubular flowers come in April and May. In each, five-petal lobes abruptly form a flat disc, each lobe separate and notched. The simple, pointed, oval leaves are in pairs along the stem. William Bartram noted "the almost endless varieties of the . . . Phlox, that enamel swelling green banks." Peter Collinson wrote of this species: "A very pale blue Lychnidea, in flower May 5th, 1740, not in England before; now in most gardens; from the Susquehana River." Blue phlox belongs to the phlox family, Polemoniaceae.

Bouncing Bet—*Saponaria officinalis*

Bouncing Bet is a stout-stemmed perennial of great vigor, which may account for its name. Other folk names — soapwort, scourwort, and latherwort — refer (as does the generic name from the Latin word *sapo,* "soap") to the use of the plant in place of soap in Europe and later in the American colonies. The bruised leaves yield a juice which makes a fair lather. The specific name, from the Latin *officina,* "workshop," also denotes practical or medicinal uses. The flowers, white to pink (occasionally deep magenta rose), about an inch across, are in large, loose, rather flat clusters. Individual petals are five notched, a common characteristic of the pink family, Caryophyllaceae. Double forms are common, both in cultivated and wild strains. The opposite leaves are lance shaped, stalkless, smooth margined, and with three prominent veins. Bouncing Bet has spread over so much of eastern America that it is generally assumed it was introduced into the colonies from England at an early date.

Cabbage rose—*Rosa centifolia*

The cabbage rose is one of the oldest of garden roses and it may even be that this species was the "many-petaled rose" of Homer or the "sixty-petaled rose" of Herodotus. Both cabbage and *centifolia* (literally, "hundred leaves") are descriptive of the large number of petals in the pink flower. For centuries, only the "very double" form has been known. This rose has five thin leaflets, usually hairy on both sides, and a stalk both prickly and bristly. The blooming date is June and later.

The cabbage rose came to England from the eastern Caucasus region in 1596. Lady Skipwith had "Marble and Cabbage Roses" in her garden at Prestwould. All roses are members of the family Rosaceae.

Calendula—*Calendula officinalis*

Calendula takes its common and generic names from the Latin *calendae,* the first days of the months, because it blooms throughout the summer. It is often known as marigold (originally Mary's gold); others prefer pot marigold—a reference to its use to season soups and stews. *Officinalis,* from *officina,* "workshop" also connotes practical uses. There are many different folk names in use in England and numerous allusions; it is probable that this is the "Mary-bud" of *Cymbeline.* The yellow or orange flower heads are 2 inches across with rather narrow "petals." The large, lance-shaped, toothless leaves are alternately arranged. According

to one record calendulas were taken to England from southern Europe in 1573. "Marigolds" were seen in the gardens of Dutch New Netherlands in 1642, in Virginia in 1650, and in 1672 Josselyn affirmed that "Marygold . . . groweth very well in New England." Calendulas belong to the calendula tribe of the family Compositae.

Canterbury bells—*Campanula medium*

Although Canterbury bells were not introduced into England, from Germany, until 1597, their English name goes back to the twelfth century when pilgrims, carrying small bells, began to make their way through fields of wild flowers (probably *C. trachelium*) to the shrine of St. Thomas à Becket in Canterbury. *Campanula* means "little bell"; *medium,* the pre-Linnaean generic name, refers to the size of the plant— sometimes as tall as 4 feet. In May and June, bell-shaped flowers, about 2 inches long and usually violet-blue, form loose, spikelike clusters. The leaves are from 6-9 inches long and hairy. Native to southern Europe, the first documented appearance of Canterbury bells in America is an advertisement in a Boston newspaper in 1760. Lady Skipwith grew this plant, which belongs to the Campanulaceae.

Carnation—*Dianthus caryophyllus*

A history of carnations, or clove pinks, would be almost a history of gardens. Introduced from Asia into Europe before historic times, the carnation was imported into England sometime before 1510, and

was the "gilliflower" of Chaucer, Spenser, and Shakespeare. *Dianthus,* "Jove's flower," was originally applied by Theophrastus to a wild pink. *Caryophyllus,* Greek for "clove tree," a pre-Linnaean name, was transferred because of the carnation's clovelike fragrance. Carnation probably derives from "coronation," since the flowers were used for wreaths and Pliny listed it as a garland plant in his *Coronamentorum.* The characteristic leaves are narrow and pale gray-green. The flowers, one to three to a stem, in color white, pink, purple, sometimes red, have five coarsely toothed or fringed petals, and a long, tubular, and often split calyx. In his *Herball* Gerard wrote: "The conserve made of the floures of the Clove Gillofloure and sugar is exceeding cordiall." He complained that there were too many kinds to describe them all. Today there are perhaps two thousand or more horticultural varieties of carnations which, with the pinks, belong to the Caryophyllaceae. References to carnations in the American colonies are frequent. One of the earliest is by Thomas Ashe in "Carolina," 1682, another by Gabriel Thomas, "West Jersey," 1698. John Bartram wrote Collinson: "I now have a glorious appearance of Carnations from thy seed . . . what with thine, Dr. Witt's and others, I can challenge any garden in America for variety." (See also grass pink.)

Carolina allspice—*Calycanthus floridus*

Carolina allspice or sweet shrub, which blooms in April and early May, has dark reddish or purplish-brown, clover-sized flowers with a strawberrylike fragrance. They are made up of similarly colored

calyx parts and petals. The leaves, 3-5 inches long and opposite, are broadly oval, narrowing abruptly to a point at the tip; dark green above, they are pale and very hairy beneath. The fruit is a dark, dry, fig-shaped receptacle full of large brown "seeds." *Calycanthus* comes from the Greek words for "calyx" and "flower"; *floridus* means "flowering." This hairy shrub, 4-8 feet high, a member of its own family Calycanthaceae, is native from Virginia to Florida and along the Gulf of Mexico. First sent to England from Carolina in 1726, Catesby figured it in his *Natural History,* and there are numerous references to it — as "Butneria," "Beureria," and "Basteria" — in the correspondence of Collinson and Bartram. John Ellis suggested to Linnaeus that he name this plant gardenia after Dr. Alexander Garden of Charleston. Both Washington and Jefferson grew it in their gardens.

Carolina jessamine—*Gelsemium sempervirens*

The native vine Carolina jessamine, or Carolina wild woodbine, bears fragrant yellow flowers in April and May. These are moderately small, funnel shaped, five lobed at the end, and grow singly or in clusters of two to six blooms at the ends of lateral branchlets. The evergreen leaves are 2 to 4 inches long, narrowly triangular, and shiny. The generic name is a Latinized version of *gelsemino,* Italian for the true jasmine (a quite different plant); *sempervirens* means "always green." Carolina jessamine was sent to England in 1640. John Banister noted it in Virginia, and it was illustrated and described in Catesby's *Natural History.* Dr. Garden, sending

seeds to John Ellis, remarked "As it is very different from the Jasminum, I design to send it to you with a new name next season." He thought Linnaeus was wrong in classifying the plant under *Bignonia.* Thomas Jefferson listed "yellow jasmine" as an ornamental, and planned to use it. The natural range is from eastern Virginia along the coast to Guatemala; it is a member of the largely tropical family Loganiaceae.

Cat-tail—*Typha latifolia*

This bog plant is readily recognized by the thick, brown spike that rises from among slender, irislike leaves. The upper portion of the spike, with minute, petaled, staminate flowers, eventually breaks off, leaving hundreds of minute, petalless, seed-producing flowers in the lower part and these, going to seed, suggest a cat's tail in fluff and thickness. *Typha* is the old Greek name for these plants, the ultimate word, *typhos,* meaning "a bog," their habitat; *latifolia* means "broad leaves" and distinguishes this from the narrow-leaved species, also grown in Williamsburg. Josselyn reported that Indians in New England ate parts of the plants. Virginia settlers were said to be "very fond" of the sweet-tasting tuberous portions. Indian women made coarse mats from the "flags," and Peter Kalm mentioned their use to prevent chafing under a horse collar. A native and cosmopolitan species known since earliest times, this cat-tail belongs to its own family, Typhaceae.

Chaste tree—*Vitex agnus-castus*

Long associated with old gardens, the chaste tree is a flowering shrub which blooms in June and July. Also known as hemp tree, monk's pepper tree, and tree of chastity, its most common name is from the Latin *castus* or "pure." In addition, the Greek *agnos,* a willowlike tree used at religious festivals, became associated with the Latin *agnus,* "holy." The whole name, *Vitex agnus-castus,* was the ancient Latin one for this or a similar shrub. The chaste tree has four-angled branches and opposite, compound leaves divided into five to seven tapering leaflets, gray and hairy beneath, all coming from the same point. Small, pale blue or lilac flowers grow in long, tapering, dense spikes. The species originated in southern Europe and Asia Minor and was brought to England from Sicily in 1570. Clayton mentioned it in *Flora Virginica,* and Jefferson in his *Garden Book.* The chaste tree belongs to the family Verbenaceae.

Cherokee rose — *Rosa laevigata*

The Cherokee rose is not native to America as the common name suggests, but was introduced into England from China as *R. sinica* in 1759. It has long been naturalized in the southern states and is the origin of the modern Silver Moon. *Laevigata*, meaning "smoothed," probably has reference to the shining leaves, subdivided into three to five singly toothed leaflets. This member of the rose family, Rosaceae, is a climber with curved thorns scattered along the stout stem. The white flowers, which bloom in May and June, are large — 3½ inches across—and solitary, each on a densely bristled pedicel. Since the Cherokee rose is now the state flower of Georgia, it is interesting to note that on April 29, 1804, Thomas Jefferson recorded that he "planted seeds of the Cherokee rose from Gov. Milledge [of Georgia] in a row . . . near the N. E. corner of the Nursery."

Cherry laurel — *Laurocerasus caroliniana*

The evergreen small tree or shrub, cherry laurel or laurel cherry, is listed in many reference books as *Prunus caroliniana*. The plant, in southern gardens, may be the American species, native to the coast, North Carolina to Texas, or it may be the now more common European species, *L. officinalis* — sometimes called English laurel. The genus, *Laurocerasus,* is the Latin for "lau-

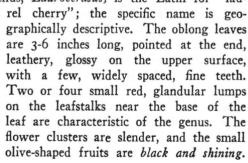

rel cherry"; the specific name is geographically descriptive. The oblong leaves are 3-6 inches long, pointed at the end, leathery, glossy on the upper surface, with a few, widely spaced, fine teeth. Two or four small red, glandular lumps on the leafstalks near the base of the leaf are characteristic of the genus. The flower clusters are slender, and the small olive-shaped fruits are *black and shining.*

(If the flower clusters are distinctly shorter than the leaves or the fruits dark purple, then the plant is probably the European cherry laurel, also known in colonial times.) Cherry laurels, members of the large rose family, Rosaceae, are too tender to grow north of Virginia.

China aster—*Callistephus chinensis*

The China, or garden, aster was sent from eastern Asia to France by the Jesuit missionary, Father d'Incarville, about 1730. Philip Miller planted seeds in England the next year and by 1752 had the

double form. In 1735, Peter Collinson sent seeds to John Bartram remarking: "It makes a glorious autumn flower. There is white and purple in the seeds." The flower heads resemble some chrysanthemums. Almost all colors except yellow or orange are known, though dark purple or shades of violet or blue are most typical. The many "petals," really ray florets, are all about the same size, long, narrow, and more or less curled at the ends. The leaves are broadly to triangularly ovate, irregularly and deeply toothed on a hairy, branching stem, about 2 feet tall. China asters bloom from July to October. The generic name is Greek for "beautiful crown"; *chinensis* is for the country of origin. The China aster belongs to the aster tribe of the family Compositae, as do members of the genus *Aster*.

Chinaberry—*Melia azedarach*

The chinaberry has other common names, among them China tree, pride of China, pride of India, and bead tree (because in some countries the hard, ridged stones are used for rosaries). *Melia* was the ancient Greek name for a somewhat similar plant; *azedarach*, a pre-Linnaean name for the species, comes from the Persian *azaddrakht*, "noble tree." The large leaves, perhaps a yard long, are repeatedly subdivided into sharp and deeply toothed, light green leaflets that give a characteristic lacy effect, yet are so numerous that considerable shade is provided. In April, lilac-colored flowers, an inch across, appear in open clusters. The fruit, resembling yellow

cherries, usually lasts all winter. The chinaberry, a member of the tropical mahogany
family, Meliaceae, reached Europe from the
Orient through Asia Minor. There is record
of its introduction into England in 1656,
though it is possible that John Gerard grew
it much earlier. On March 14, 1778,
Thomas Jefferson planted "Pride of China"
in his nursery. Travelers just after the
Revolution noted it in Virginia and the
Carolinas. A flat-topped variety, often called the umbrella tree, *M.
azedarach umbraculiformis,* probably was unknown to the colonists.

Clematis—*Clematis virginiana*

This clematis is a vine native to North America east of the Rockies.
Other names include virgin's bower, old-man's-beard, devil's hair,
wild hops, and traveler's joy (the name common in England for
another species, *C. vitalba*). *Clematis* was Dioscorides' name for a
vine with slender branches; *virginiana* refers to the botanical
region — more extensive than the present commonwealth — from
which the plant was first collected, although it grew wild or probably
was cultivated in all the original thirteen colonies. The opposite
leaves, divided into three leaflets, are oval
and coarsely toothed; the sensitive leafstalks
twine on contact. Blooming in midsummer,
the white flowers grow in profusion in flat-
topped, lacy clusters. The "petals," really
sepals, form a cross and there are numerous
stamens. The fruits are gray and plumed
with feathery threads. Clematis belongs to
the large buttercup family, Ranunculaceae.
The first record of its cultivation is in 1720,
and it was sent to England in 1767. Thomas
Walter mentioned it in his *Flora Caroliniana.*

Cockscomb—*Celosia argentea cristata*

Cockscomb is so called because the flat, distorted flower clusters
resemble poultry combs in shape, and sometimes in color. The generic
name, from the Greek *kelos,* "burned," may refer to the texture, and

perhaps color, of the flowers; *argentea* means "silvery," and alludes to the Asiatic weed of which this is a variety. Minute flowers are densely crowded on either flattened and fan-like, or conical and spearlike flower heads. Such bizarre shapes result from distortions of the growing point or apical meristem. They are technically known as fasciation and occur, less regularly, in other plants. When the apical meristem is divided into separate points, each flower head becomes a series of subdivided, flower-covered, plumose spikes. This form, *plumosa,* is also *cristata,* not a separate variety. (But it is not unlikely that the variety *cristata* may yet be elevated to specific rank.) Blooming from July until late October, cockscomb flowers are dull red-purple or yellow-orange. Three forms were introduced into England from Asia in 1570. In 1709, John Lawson noted "Prince's feather very large and beautiful" in the gardens of Carolina. The Perry letters of 1739 note it in Virginia, and William Beverley ordered seeds of "Amar. Coxcomb." In 1760, "Indian Branching cockscombs" were listed for sale in Boston. Thomas Jefferson sowed "cockscomb, a flower like the Prince's feather." The plant belongs to the amaranth family, Amaranthaceae.

Columbine—*Aquilegia canadensis*

This wild columbine, a member of the buttercup family, Ranunculaceae, is a native of central and eastern North America. The specific name refers to the general region north of Virginia. The common name, from the Latin *columba,* "dove," is of uncertain origin; *aquilegia* is also puzzling, since the nearest Latin word, *aquilegus,* means "water drawer." Some, however, derive it from *aquila,* "eagle," because of the flower's five talonlike spurs, bulb tipped, backward pointing, and each about an inch long; these, filled with nectar, account for another common name, honeysuckle (not of course to be confused with *Lonicera*). Numerous stamens protrude almost as far in the opposite directions. The flowers, scarlet-red without and yellowish within,

26

droop singly or in small clusters. The buttercuplike leaves are bluntly lobed and toothed. The son of John Tradescant, gardener to Charles I, forwarded columbine plants to Hampton Court from Virginia in 1640. Josselyn noted the plant in New England where Indians drank infusions of the seeds for headaches. Collinson wrote Bartram "Thy Columbine is in flower, which is earlier than any we have by two months." Jefferson and Lady Skipwith both grew it.

Common catalpa—*Catalpa bignonioides*

The common catalpa, native to the Gulf states, has long been naturalized as far north as New York. The Cherokee Indian name, of which catawba is a variant, was Latinized into *catalpa; bignonioides,* "bignonialike," suggests the resemblance to that related genus within the same largely tropical family, Bignoniaceae. The catalpa is also called the Indian bean-tree, cigar tree, and smoking-bean-tree, names which reflect the belief that the Indians smoked the foot-long, very thin, cylindrical pods and their papery winged seeds. The large, broadly heart-shaped or triangular leaves end in a distinct tapering point; they grow in twos and threes from the stout twigs. Foot-long clusters of trumpet-shaped flowers — white, thickly spotted with purple-brown, and having yellow dots within—appear in June. The bark is thin and scaly in contrast to the thick and ridged bark of the western catalpa, also seen in Williamsburg. Discovered by Mark Catesby, the common catalpa was introduced into England in 1726. John Bartram and Dr. Garden also mentioned it.

Coralberry—*Symphoricarpos orbiculatus*

The coralberry or Indian currant is a native low shrub ranging from New Jersey to Georgia and westward to Texas, Kansas, and South Dakota. The generic name, from the Greek words *symphorein,* "to bring together," and *karpos,* "fruit," refers to the densely clustered berries; *orbiculatus,* "circular" or "globular," is descriptive of the shape of the fruit. The short-stalked, small, oval leaves are opposite. The numerous small, white, bell-shaped flowers along and

at the ends of the stems, bloom in June or July. These are followed by small, dull, purplish-red, persistent berries — the plant's most distinctive feature. They grow in dense clusters, and are so numerous they conceal the wood. First recorded in cultivation in 1727, coralberry was sent to England in 1730. John Bartram listed "Symphoricarpos orbiculatus" in his catalogue, and John Clayton believed the powdered root, taken internally, to be "an infallible remedy against intermittent fever." He refers to malaria, which was such a scourge to early settlers in Virginia. Coralberry belongs to the honeysuckle family, Caprifoliaceae.

Coreopsis—*Coreopsis lanceolata*

This coreopsis, also called tickseed and garden and lance-leaved tickseed, is a native of eastern North America that has been cultivated for a long time. The long blooming period— throughout the summer — and general ease of cultivation doubtless were factors in this. Coreopsis was sent to England from "Carolina" in 1724. In his *Flora Caroliniana* Walter mentioned seven kinds of coreopsis of which four are native species still more or less cultivated. The flower heads, on very long stalks, have notched, pure yellow "petals" and yellow discs. The leaves, principally basal, may have quite separate and elongated divisions, but for the most part are lance shaped and undivided. The common and generic name is from the Greek *koris,* "bug," and *opsis,* "appearance," an allusion to the shape, size, and color of the oval, dry fruits; *lanceolata* refers to the lance-shaped foliage. The plant is a member of the sunflower tribe of the family Compositae.

Cornelian cherry—*Cornus mas*

The cornelian cherry, a small tree, is also called European dogwood and cornel. *Cornus* is from *cornolium,* the Latin name for this species, the ultimate source being *cornus,* "horn," in reference to the hard wood; *mas,* "masculine," is obscure except that in ancient times the qualities of one sex or the other were ascribed to some plants. Cornelian cherry has three to five pairs of branch veins parallel with the leaf margin, a characteristic of members of the dogwood family, Cornaceae. The opposite leaves, green on both sides, differ from those of the flowering dogwood, the leaves of which are  whitish underneath. The small, yellowish flowers appear in dense clusters in March or April; the large, cherrylike, acid fruits are ripe in August. The plant figures in Greek and Roman mythology and the earliest record of it goes back to 1072 B.C. As "Cornus mascula," it was introduced into England from Austria in 1596. Adrian Van der Donck, who settled in Dutch New Amsterdam in 1642, and after whom Yonkers is named, imported the cornelian cherry from Holland.

Cornflower—*Centaurea cyanus*

The cornflower is so called because in Europe it grows wild in the fields of "corn" or grain (not maize). It is also known as bachelor's button, bluebottle, and bluebonnet — all names applied to several other plants. The genus is from the centaur of Greek mythology, Chiron, who used the plant to allay the pain of the wound  made by the arrow of Hercules poisoned by the blood of the Hydra; *cyanus* is from the Greek *kyanos,* "dark blue." Gerard grew the "Blew-Bottle or Corne-Floure" and in his time it was also known as hurt-sickle because it was thought it blunted the blades at harvest. The cornflower blooms in May through summer. The deep blue or purple, sometimes pink or white, flowers, with tubular "petals" (really individual florets), attached to a convex solitary flower head, are borne on a stalk, naked at the top, with small, grasslike leaves lower down. In *Gardens of Colony and State* this member of the thistle tribe of the family Compositae is said to have reached America between 1700 and 1750; it is mentioned in Walter's *Flora Caroliniana.*

Crape myrtle—*Lagerstroemia indica*

The crape myrtle is a tall shrub or small tree, striking when it is in bloom from late June or July, through most of the summer. The common name comes from the crapelike flower petals and the resemblance of the leaves to the true myrtle, *Myrtus communis*. Linnaeus named the genus for his friend, Magnus von Lagerstroem, a merchant of Gottenburg. The bark of the older stems has a piebald effect of dark patches on pale olive green. The small, almost stalkless, leaves are narrowly oval, 1-2 inches, mostly opposite. Fringed or crinkled six-petaled flowers terminate each twig in prominent, long-lasting clusters. Predominant shades are pink and blush pink but purple and white also occur. The small, green seed capsules become brown and woody then open, usually into six parts, and remain until the following summer. The species, of the lythrum family, Lythryaceae, was introduced into Europe from India and China in 1747, and is also recorded as having been imported into England from the East Indies in 1759. It was listed in the Elgin Botanical Garden, New York, in 1811, and it could have arrived in America before the end of the eighteenth century.

Crocus—*Crocus vernus*

The crocus bears one of the oldest names in the plant world. *Krokos* was given to *C. sativus,* or saffron, in the third century B.C. by Theophrastus; *vernus,* "spring," indicates that this variety (like most, but not all, crocuses) blooms in that season—in Williamsburg March or earlier. Originally from southern Europe, it has been cultivated all over Europe so long that there are no records of its introduction into England. William Byrd I mentioned the crocus in letters dated 1683 and 1684. Peter Collinson sent more than twenty varieties to John Bartram in 1740, "such a collection as is rarely met with, all at once." *C. vernus* bears open, cup-shaped flowers with six erect perianth segments (three petals, three sepals, similarly colored). White, lilac, lavender, blue, purple, and red-purple in color, the blooms are sometimes plain, sometimes striped. The two to four narrow leaves have a white middle line; there is no visible stem. This crocus, originally from Southern Europe, is a member of the iris family, Iridaceae. (See also fall crocus.)

Cross-vine—*Bignonia capreolata*

Cross-vine is a native species ranging from Virginia to Florida and westward. The common name refers to the four areas visible in a cross section of the stem and not to the paired leafstalks which
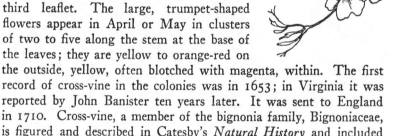
form horizontal lines at right angles to the stem. The genus was named for Abbé Jean Paul Bignon, court librarian to Louis XIV; *capreolata* means "bearing tendrils." The vine has evergreen, opposite leafstalks, each of which forks into two elongate-oval leaflets 3-5 inches long, and has a branched tendril with small, adhesive discs, really a modified third leaflet. The large, trumpet-shaped flowers appear in April or May in clusters of two to five along the stem at the base of the leaves; they are yellow to orange-red on the outside, yellow, often blotched with magenta, within. The first record of cross-vine in the colonies was in 1653; in Virginia it was reported by John Banister ten years later. It was sent to England in 1710. Cross-vine, a member of the bignonia family, Bignoniaceae, is figured and described in Catesby's *Natural History* and included in Walter's *Flora Caroliniana* and John Bartram's catalogue.

Daffodil—*Narcissus pseudo-narcissus*

The daffodil, native to Europe and England, has a trumpet as long as, or longer than, the perianth segments; the leaves are flat and bladelike. The common name may be a corruption of "saffron lily" or of "asphodel," which was the poet's narcissus, *N. poeticus;* or it may be from the Old English *affodyle,* "that which comes early," for it is a flower of early spring, blooming in March or April. The generic name comes from the well-known myth of Narcissus (see jonquil). The specific name distinguishes this from other species in the genus. There are many folk names in the British Isles, including variants of daffydowndilly and affradil. Collinson esteemed it a special favor when he sent seeds of the double white daffodil to Bartram, and was surprised to learn in reply that the first settlers had taken bulbs with them, which had multiplied "so that thousands are thrown away."

The daffodil is a member of the amaryllis family, Amaryllidaceae, which includes the jonquil, narcissus, fall daffodil, and snowdrop.

Edging box– *Buxus sempervirens suffruticosa*

Dwarf box, Dutch box, and slow box (because of its slow growth) are other common names for this much valued shrub. It is distinguished from tree box by its smaller oval leaves—¼-½ inch long,

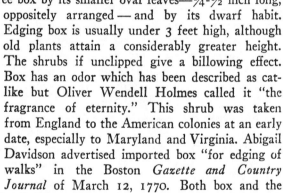

oppositely arranged — and by its dwarf habit. Edging box is usually under 3 feet high, although old plants attain a considerably greater height. The shrubs if unclipped give a billowing effect. Box has an odor which has been described as cat-like but Oliver Wendell Holmes called it "the fragrance of eternity." This shrub was taken from England to the American colonies at an early date, especially to Maryland and Virginia. Abigail Davidson advertised imported box "for edging of walks" in the Boston *Gazette and Country Journal* of March 12, 1770. Both box and the genus are from the Latin *buxus,* the Greek *puxos,* names for this plant; *sempervirens,* "evergreen," and *suffruticosa,* "somewhat shrubby," complete the nomenclature. Originally from southern Europe, northern Africa, and western Asia, box belongs to its own family, Buxaceae.

Elder –*Sambucus canadensis*

This elder or elderberry is a native shrub ranging over most of the North American continent east of the Rockies. "Elder" derives from the Anglo-Saxon *ellen,* "fire-kindler"; *sambucus* is the classical

Latin name for the elder, and *canadensis* refers to the general botanical region, north of Virginia, where the plant was first collected. Flat-topped clusters of small white flowers appear in May or June; small, dark purple, edible berries, which bend the slender stems with their weight, are ripe in August. The opposite, compound leaves are divided into five to eleven finely saw-toothed leaflets that resemble peach leaves. The colonists, like the Indians, ate the fruit, brewed the leaves for tea, and made elderberry wine and jelly. From the twigs, which readily lose their white pith, boys fashioned whistles and pop guns, their fathers spiles for tapping sugar maples. Peter Kalm found the Iroquois boiling the inner bark for a toothache poultice. The elder belongs to the honeysuckle family, Caprifoliaceae.

English daisy—*Bellis perennis*

The word "daisy," from the Anglo-Saxon *daeges eage,* "day's eye," was coined centuries ago. This flower is the "eye of day" of Chaucer, the "bright dayes-eyes" of Jonson, and the daisy of Spenser, Bacon, and Shakespeare. Common names, too numerous to list in full, include bachelor's button, bairnwort, gowan, herb Margaret, and measure-of-love. *Bellis* means "pretty"; *perennis,* "perennial." This plant is low and dandelionlike, but the leaves in the basal rosette are not finely cut. In the original the flower is single, with flower heads — white edged or tinged with red, as described by Pliny the Elder — growing on slender, hairy stalks. Double varieties, where the central disc has dwindled to the vanishing point and the color is all red, date at least from 1597 when Gerard wrote "The double daisies are planted in gardens; the others grow wilde everywhere." This beloved inhabitant of English meadows, a member of the aster tribe of the family Compositae, has been taken by Englishmen wherever they go.

English ivy—*Hedera helix*

English ivy is the ivy of literature and tradition. In the days of ancient Greece it was sacred to Dionysos. The name "ivy" is from *ifig,* Anglo-Saxon word for the species; *hedera* is the classical Latin

name; *helix,* Greek for "spiral," suggests the vine's habit of growth. Peter Kalm noted English ivy growing on a building in Philadelphia. Jefferson grew it at Monticello, and Washington mentions it in his diary of 1785. The vine is evergreen, with dark, waxy, three- or four-lobed leaves that have conspicuous white or yellow veins; the stems have dense tufts of aerial roots at short intervals. The plants generally retain the juvenile condition of lobed leaves, but occasionally, on parts of the vine that may be flowering, the leaves are more or less heart shaped. This European plant is a member of the ginseng family, Araliaceae.

English primrose—*Primula vulgaris*

The English primrose is an early spring flower. This is reflected both in the common name and the generic *primula,* diminutive of the Latin *primus,* "first." The Latin *vulgaris* means "abundant" or "common." The wrinkled, broadly lance-shaped leaves are 3-5 inches long, have wavy margins, and grow in a basal rosette. The flowers,

which bloom in April in Williamsburg, are light yellow, rarely purple or blue, and have no central "eye," as does the cowslip, *P. veris,* and the auriculas. Primroses are native to England and Gerard grew them in his London garden. In his Account Book of 1771, Thomas Jefferson planned for "primrose" in his garden at Monticello. Lady Skipwith had both "cowslip" and "English cowslip" at Prestwould, indicating that she probably had both this species and *P. veris.* Primroses are members of the primrose family, Primulaceae.

34

English yew — *Taxus baccata*

English yew, a handsome, slow-growing, evergreen tree, is not aromatic as are most conifers. It bears scarlet, berrylike, modified cones. The soft, dark green needles, 1-2 inches long and yellow-gray underneath, grow in horizontal rows. The juice of both fruit and foliage is dangerously poisonous. "Yew" is from the Anglo-Saxon name of this species, *iw; taxus,* the Latin, is from the Greek name for this plant, *taxos; baccata* means "berried." The yew is native to England where it is associated with churchyards. Varieties of yew have been cultivated for centuries in most parts of Europe. It is probable that trees were introduced into colonial America in many instances in which records have not yet been found. John Custis ordered yew for his  garden in Williamsburg in 1717. Clayton reported it in Virginia in 1764, and in 1771 Jefferson planned to plant yew. English yew, which belongs to the yew family, Taxaceae, does not do well in much of Virginia, and other evergreens were early substituted for it.

Fall crocus — *Crocus speciosus*

Fall crocus, which blooms in August and not in the spring when most of its relatives do, has blue-purple or lavender, open, cup-shaped flowers with no visible stem. The six erect perianth segments (three petals and three sepals) are similarly colored. The leaves, usually three, appear with or soon after the flowers. True fall crocuses have

three stamens; the lavender autumn crocus, a colchicum, has *six* stamens. The common and generic names are derived from *krokos,* the Greek name given to saffron (*C. sativus*) by Theophrastus in the third century B.C. *Speciosus,* from the Latin, means "showy" or "conspicuous." The introduction of this species into Europe from the Caucasus region of Asia apparently was early, although the exact date is not known. In 1754, William Logan of Germantown, Pennsylvania, ordered "100 yellow and blue crocuces that blow in the fall of the year." Fall crocus belongs to the iris family, Iridaceae. (See also crocus and autumn crocus.)

Fall daffodil—*Sternbergia lutea*

Fall daffodil resembles the daffodil only in color—it has neither cup nor trumpet. Named for Count Caspar Sternberg, a botanist and author of Prague, it is variously known as sternbergia, winter daffodil, and fall crocus. *Lutea* is Latin for "yellow." The erect, cup-shaped, crocus-like flowers open in August and September, usually solitary, on a stem 4-7 inches tall. The six perianth segments are prominently veined. Six to eight long narrow leaves are present. The orange-yellow fall daffodil will not be confused with the lavender fall crocus or with the lavender autumn crocus, a colchicum. Fall daffodil, a member of the amaryllis family, Amaryllidaceae, was introduced into England in 1596 from southern Europe, and presumably was imported into this country at an early date. It was included in Lady Skipwith's garden record as "Yellow Autumn Amaryllis-Daffodil."

Fig—*Ficus carica*

The edible fig, a member of the mulberry family, Moraceae, is one of the oldest plants known, cultivated for at least 4,000 years. (The fig of the Bible is probably *F. sycomorus*.) There is a botanical record of the fig's importation into England in 1548, but it may have been grown there as early as Roman times. With other fruits, it was introduced in the colonies from the beginning, and records are numerous. In 1629, a Mrs. Pearce reported that, from her three or four acre garden at Jamestown, she had gathered in one year a hundred bushels of figs. The form grown as an ornamental in Williamsburg is more shrub than tree, with clumps of stout, soft-looking stems. The three- to five-lobed leaves are large and hairy; the pear-shaped fruit, 2 or 3 inches

36

long, is a hollow receptacle without seeds, since the plants are not cross-pollinated. "Fig," through the French *figue* and the Provençal *figa,* is from the Latin name, *ficus,* which may be derived originally from the Hebrew *feg; carica* pertains to Caria, a region of southwest Asia Minor, thought to be the original home of the species.

Flame azalea—*Rhododendron calendulaceum*

The flame azalea was described by William Bartram as "the most gay and brilliant flowering shrub yet known." William's father, John, believed he was the first to discover the plant, in 1749, in New York State. The general range of this native of the Appalachians is from Pennsylvania to Georgia and westward to Ohio and Kentucky. Azalea is from the Greek, *azaleos,* "dry" (because the plant was supposed to flourish in dry ground). *Rhododendron,* from the Greek, is literally "rose-red tree"; *calendulaceum,* or "calendulalike," refers to the flower's yellow or orange color. Fire azalea is another common name. The shrub, a member of the large heath family, Ericaceae, grows from 5-10 feet high. Clusters of about six yellow-orange, sometimes red, flowers appear in May. These are large and trumpet shaped, sticky-hairy on the outside, with stamens projecting prominently against a background of the plants own, just-growing leaves.

Flowering dogwood—*Cornus florida*

The button-shaped flower buds of dogwood open in April or early May into four large, notched, petallike leaves—white, sometimes pink—which surround the true flowers, small and greenish white to yellow. These true flowers appear before the leaves, or bracts, and remain for several weeks as the colored bracts conclude development. The foliage leaves, whitish beneath, are opposite with five to seven pairs of veins parallel with the leaf margin. In older trees the bark is checkered. "Dogwood" may have originated from the European use of the fine-grained wood for meat skewers or daggers — hence dagwood, or dogwood. The generic name comes from *cornolium,* Latin for the European cornelian cherry (a member of the same family,

Cornaceae), and derives originally from *cornus*, "horn," referring to the hardness of the wood; *florida* means "full of flowers." This species, which is native to the eastern United States, was well known to the colonists, who used the frayed twigs as toothbrushes. William Byrd thought the bark a specific for malaria; when he ran the Dividing Line between Virginia and North Carolina he wrote: "Our chief medicine was Dogwood bark, which we used instead of that of Peru." As "Cornus mas virginiana," Catesby described flowering dogwood in his *Natural History* and reported finding, in Virginia, a dogwood with "flowers of a rose-colour." He sent both pink and white dogwood to Fairchild in London in 1731.

Foamflower—*Tiarella cordifolia*

Foamflower, a native herbaceous plant growing in rich woodlands from Nova Scotia to Georgia, may well have ornamented colonial gardens. The common name has reference to the small white flowers,

scarcely ¼ inch across, that bloom during April and May in dense, spike-shaped clusters at the end of flower stalks 6-12 inches high. The ten tiny orange anthers are conspicuous. Linnaeus chose *tiarella,* the diminutive of "tiara"—which comes through the Latin and Greek from a Persian word for a turban—because of the general shape and cleft character of the seed case; *cordifolia* describes the heart-shaped leaves which are broad, hairy, lobed, and coarsely toothed. Other common names are false miterwort (from its resemblance to its relatives, the true miterworts), coolwort, and Nancy-over-the-ground. This dainty garden plant, a member of the family Saxifragaceae, was introduced into England in 1731.

Four-o'clock—*Mirabilis jalapa*

True to their name, four-o'clocks, or afternoon ladies, open mostly late in the afternoon (earlier in cloudy weather) and close in the

morning. Another common name, marvel-of-Peru, commemorates the impression made when this plant was brought to England from the West Indies in 1596. Linnaeus derived the generic name from a Latin adjective meaning "wonderful" or "strange"; *jalapa* refers to the erroneous belief that the roots contained jalap, a powerful purge—hence also the name false jalap. The flowers, in bloom from midsummer to fall, have long, slender, tapering corolla tubes, broadly flaring at the end. Their colors are white, purple, yellow, and shades of red, often streaked or striped. The paired, oval to triangular foliage leaves, are rather short stalked. Thomas Jefferson noted on July 18, 1767, "Mirabilis just opened, very clever." Native to Mexico, Central America, and the West Indies, the plant belongs to the four-o'clock family, Nyctaginaceae.

Foxglove—*Digitalis purpurea*

The foxglove is one of England's native plants, grown in the earliest gardens. Folk names are too numerous to list; most of them refer to the fingerlike shape of the corolla — fairy fingers, folks' gloves, and lady's thimble — as does the Latin *digitalis; purpurea,* "purple," indicates the color of the flowers, purple to purplish pink or white. These bloom in June in a long, one-sided cluster; the downward-pointing, bell-shaped flowers are 2-3 inches long, usually spotted within, and have only four stamens (unlike campanulas which have five). Gerard the herbalist, who catalogued the "vertues" of plants and ascribed supposed medicinal properties to so many, was unaware that this member of the snapdragon family, Scrophulariaceae, is the source of the important drug digitalin, often prescribed for tired hearts. Under its present name, foxglove was mentioned about 1440 in Mayster John Gardener's *Feate of Gardening*. In all probability it was introduced into America at an early date, but no record has been found prior to 1748, when Peter Kalm found it blooming as late as October 18 in Philadelphia.

Fox grape—*Vitis labrusca*

This native vine with a foxlike odor has leaves which are broad, heart shaped at the base, and irregularly or slightly three lobed and toothed, 3-7 inches long; the lower surface is usually rusty-hairy. The plant climbs by forked tendrils. The word "grape" comes ultimately from the old Germanic *chrapho*, "hook"; *vitis* was the Latin name for the wine grape (*V. vinifera*), the "vine" of the Bible; *labrusca* refers to the Latin name for some wild vine, not necessarily a grape. After many unsuccessful attempts to cultivate the European grape, the colonists turned to this purplish-black wild species which impressed them with its vigor. It became a source of table grapes, jelly, and wine. On October 12, 1728, when William Byrd was running the Dividing Line between Virginia and North Carolina, he reported he had "drunk tolerably good wine prest from them." Selection and hybridization culminated, in the nineteenth century, in established varieties, including the famous Concord grape, and the Isabella and Delaware varieties. The range of the fox grape is from New England to central Georgia and westward to Southern Indiana and Tennessee. With other wild species, it belongs to the grape family, Vitaceae.

Fragrant sumac—*Rhus canadensis*

The fragrant sumac — also called aromatic, and sweet-scented, sumac — is a low shrub, 2-4 feet tall. The small, catkinlike, dense flower clusters bloom in April and May before the leaves expand. The leaflets, three in number, are 2-3 inches long, coarsely toothed and scalloped. The stiff, fuzzy, *red* fruits resemble those of most other sumacs; the native poisonous sumacs have *white* fruits. Sumac comes from the Arabic *summaq,* for a closely related plant. The generic *Rhus* comes through the Latin from the Greek *rhous,* their name for the

European smoke tree, once *Rhus cotinus,* now *Cotinus coggygria; canadensis* refers to the general botanical region north of Virginia. The records of John Banister, Thomas Jefferson, and others indicate that this sumac was planted ornamentally in colonial gardens. It belongs to the cashew family, Anacardiaceae.

French marigold—*Tagetes patula*

French marigold is a misnomer, for this familiar garden plant is a native of Mexico. Marigold is a corruption of Mary's gold, and has been applied to various yellow-flowered plants in bloom at the time of the festivals of the Virgin. *Tagetes* may come from Tages, the Etruscan deity; *patula,* "spreading," suggests the growth habit of this dwarf bushy plant, about a foot high. The moderate-sized, yellow or orange, single or double flower heads, with few to many, more or less crinkled, velvety "petals" (really ray florets), are marked with red or brown. They bloom from July late into the fall. The leaves, opposite and much divided, are strongly scented. French marigolds came to England from Mexico in 1573, according to  Sweet's *Hortus Brittanicus* and other records. Double forms are as old as the single ones; William Logan of Germantown ordered both French and African marigolds in 1749, and his instructions are indicative of the perils of the voyage: "Take care the mise don't Eat them & keep them from stormy weather . . . don't lett the Salt Water wash them." Minton Collins, a dealer in Richmond, sold "striped French Marygold" to Sir Peyton Skipwith, March 1, 1793. (See also African marigold.)

French mulberry—*Callicarpa americana*

This native species, ranging from Virginia to Texas, is neither French nor a mulberry; it slightly resembles some true members of the mulberry family, but only in the striking magenta color of the berries which crowd the stems at short intervals. They ripen in September and may persist during the winter, though cardinals, mocking birds, and thrushes are very fond of them. Other common names include Bermuda mulberry, beautyberry, and callicarpa—which is also the

generic name, from the Greek for "beautiful fruit." This shrub, 4-5 feet high, has opposite, sometimes whorled, leaves, long, triangular, 4-6 inches, gradually tapering and sharply pointed, with blunt teeth. The flowers, in June and July, are small, tubular, pale blue, and clustered in the angles of leaves and stems. First sent to England in 1724, the French mulberry was included by Catesby in his *Natural History,* and was grown by John Bartram and Thomas Jefferson. The Alabama Indians used it for malaria and the Choctaws for dysentery. It is a member of the verbena family, Verbenaceae.

Fringe-tree—*Chionanthus virginica*

In May this small tree bears white flowers, each with four very narrow, fringelike petals, which hang in numerous loose clusters, 4-8 inches long. Like a great snowy net, they cover the unfolding pale green leaves, which are roundish, but somewhat pointed at each end, untoothed, glossy, and opposite. The fruit is green, turning to bluish-black in August. *Chionanthus* is from the Greek, *chion,* "snow," and *anthos,* "a flower"; *virginica* refers to the general region, larger than the present commonwealth, in which the plant was first collected. American fringe, flowering ash, and snowflower tree are some other common names. The fringe-tree was introduced into England in 1736. References are numerous: Catesby's *Natural History* includes it; a German botanist, Dillenius, received seeds from America; Garden sent seeds to Ellis repeatedly; and Collinson wrote Cadwallader Colden he had obtained it from John Clayton in Virginia. Washington prized it and Jefferson lists the "Fringe, or snow-drop tree. Chionanthus Virginica" as an ornamental in *Notes on the State of Virginia.* In colonial times the bark of the roots was used as a laxative, a tonic, and, in Florida, as a fever medicine for dengue. Fringe-tree, a member of the olive family, Oleaceae, ranges sparsely from Pennsylvania to Florida.

Galax—*Galax aphylla*

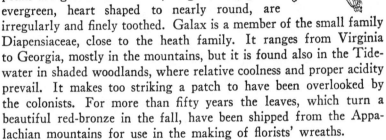

The word "galax" is from *gala,* Greek for "milk," perhaps in reference to the whiteness of the small flowers; *aphylla,* "without leaves," alludes to the leafless stalk. Known also as beetleweed and colt's foot (much better applied to the European weed, *Tussilago farfara*), galax flowers in May in a plantainlike spike at the end of a stalk 12-30 inches high. The sepals outside the petals are green. The leaves, long stalked, glossy, evergreen, heart shaped to nearly round, are irregularly and finely toothed. Galax is a member of the small family Diapensiaceae, close to the heath family. It ranges from Virginia to Georgia, mostly in the mountains, but it is found also in the Tidewater in shaded woodlands, where relative coolness and proper acidity prevail. It makes too striking a patch to have been overlooked by the colonists. For more than fifty years the leaves, which turn a beautiful red-bronze in the fall, have been shipped from the Appalachian mountains for use in the making of florists' wreaths.

Germander—*Teucrium chamaedrys*

Germander is a low, running, evergreen plant, with ovalish leaves oppositely arranged, about ¾ inch long. The small, rose to light red-purple flowers appear in June or July, and bloom through the summer in loose, spikelike clusters. The plant resembles a small box cutting, but has the mintlike flowers characteristic of the large mint family, Labiatae, to which it belongs. Germander is derived from *chamaedrys,* the Greek name for some member of this group, ultimately from *chamai,* "on the ground," and *drys,* "tree"; *Teucrium* is an old Greek word for an herb—possibly the same as the present genus — named for King Teucer, the legendary first king of Troy. A native of most of Europe and western Asia, germander was well known in England; Gerard grew it in his London garden and Francis Bacon deemed it suitable for his winter garden. It is assumed that it was introduced into the colonies at an early date.

Golden ragwort—*Senecio aureus*

Golden ragwort owes its name to the color of the flowers, and to the cut appearance of the upper leaves. *Senecio,* from the Latin name for plants of this group, is derived from *senex,* "old" or "old man," possibly because of the hoary appearance of the dry fruits; *aureus* means "golden." Common names include groundsel, liferoot, and swamp squawweed. Blooming in April or May, the individual yellow flower heads are small, about ¾ inch across, each with eight to twelve narrow "petals." They form a flat-topped terminal cluster on the green, often purplish, stem, 1-2 feet high. The long-stalked, basal leaves are heart shaped and coarsely toothed. This common native species, which ranges over eastern North America, was mentioned by John Banister, by John Clayton in his *Flora Virginica,* and in Walter's *Flora Caroliniana.* Golden ragwort is very common around Williamsburg; it is but one species of the largest genus of the plant kingdom and belongs to the ragwort tribe of the very large family Compositae.

Grape hyacinth—*Muscari botryoides*

This bulbous herb has a dense spike of small, bottle-shaped, deep blue-purple flowers that hang downward at the top of a bare flower stalk; it blooms in April and May. The common name is suggested by the grapelike cluster of flowers, and by the plant's close relation on the true hyacinth. *Muscari* is from the Latin, *muscus,* "musky" (one variety has a musky odor); *botryoides* is from the Greek *botrys,* "a  cluster," and the suffix -*oides,* "like." The leaves, ¼ inch wide, are relatively erect. (If the leaves are narrower and *bend,* and the flowers rather longer than wide, the plant is *M. racemosum,* now widely escaped around Williamsburg.) The "Grape Flowers or Muscary" mentioned in *Gardens of Colony and State* as growing before 1700, were probably *M. botryoides*. Jefferson refers to this species, and Lady Skipwith mentions grape hyacinth in her garden notes. Originally an introduced species from southern Europe, this grape hyacinth is now an escape from New Hampshire to Ohio and Virginia. It belongs to the large lily family, Liliaceae.

Grass pink—*Dianthus plumarius*

Pinks derive their name, according to Prior, from *pinksten* or *pfingsten,* the German name for pink flowers that bloomed at Pentecost, or Whitsuntide; hence the color is named for the flowers rather than the other way round. *Dianthus,*  literally "Jove's flower," from the Greek *dios,* "divine," *anthos,* "flower," was applied by Theophrastus to a wild pink, perhaps this very species; *plumarius,* from the Latin *pluma,* "feather," refers to the leaves. The plant is low and mat forming with very narrow, bluish gray-green and powdery leaves which grow in dense tufts. The flowers, in May and June, are pinkish to purple or white, finely fringed and with ten stamens. There is one record of the introduction of this plant to England from southern Europe, in 1629, but Gerard in his *Herball* described grass-leaved pinks in 1547. Grass pinks were advertised for sale in a Boston newspaper in 1760, and Thomas Jefferson mentioned them repeatedly. Lady Skipwith had "pinks of various kinds, very fine." Like the carnation, this species belongs to the pink family, Caryophyllaceae, and has a similar clovelike odor. Gerard spoke of it as "of a most fragrant smell, not inferior to the Clove Gillofloure."

Groundsel tree—*Baccharis halimifolia*

The groundsel tree, also called groundsel bush or groundsel, is a large shrub with its stems longitudinally ridged; the twigs and the lower surface of the oblong, more or less coarsely toothed leaves, are marked with numerous yellow, resinous dots. The flowers, appearing in September, are yellowish or grayish white and grow in dense clusters of small heads about ¼-inch long; the fruits, cottony and dandelionlike, are distributed by the wind. The plant is named for

its resemblance to the English groundsel, *Senecio vulgaris;* the word "groundsel" is of obscure origin, but apparently comes from the Anglo-Saxon *grunds welgie,* which means "ground glutton" or "ground swallow." *Baccharis* is from the Latin name for some fragrant-rooted plant dedicated to Bacchus; *halimifolia* means "leaves like Halimium," a genus not of garden interest. Groundsel tree, one of the few woody members of the great family Compositae, is a native of the Eastern United States from New England southward along the coast. It was first sent to England in 1683. Groundsel tree, sent to Collinson from Cape May in 1741 by John Bartram, was grown by Lord Petre as "Senecio arborescens." Dr. Garden also sent it to Ellis.

Hackberry—*Celtis occidentalis*

Hackberry is a corruption of hedgeberry. The generic *Celtis* was Pliny's name for some species of African lotus tree, probably *C. australis,* but, if not, then transferred because some hackberries also have a sweet fruit; *occidentalis* means "western" and is suited to this tree as a native of the United States. Other common names are nettle tree, sugar berry, hoop ash, hack tree, and lotus tree. The leaves, with three prominent veins, are oblique at the base, and, like the leaves of the related elms, usually saw toothed. The fruit, an orange berry that turns purplish, was dried by the Dakota Indians and used in powdered form to season meat. First introduced into England in 1656, the hackberry was grown by Peter Collinson who wrote John Bartram he had two kinds of American hackberries, one from Virginia. (The other probably was the southern species, *C. laevigata.* Several trees are to be seen near the site of the First Theatre in Williamsburg.) Hackberry was used as a corner tree by surveyors of the Virginia-North Carolina Dividing Line; it was noted by Kalm in Philadelphia and William Bartram in Florida. Hackberries belong to the elm family, Ulmaceae.

Hemlock—*Tsuga canadensis*

The common or eastern hemlock, a native member of the pine family, Pinaceae, is identified by its short, ¾-inch needles, whitish underneath, in horizontal rows with a few additional ones on top of, or parallel with, the twigs. It is used for hedges and topiary work in the Palace Garden at Williamsburg. "Hemlock" has been transferred from the name of the European (quite different) plant, *Conium maculatum,* an extract of which Socrates drank; the genus is the Latinized Japanese name for an Asiatic hemlock; *canadensis* refers to the general region—eastern United States—in which the

hemlock ranges and was first collected botanically. Josselyn noted that the bark was used by New England fishermen to dye their sails and nets, and that its turpentine was good for "any Ach." The Indians made tea from the young tips and boiled the bark of young trees for a poultice after pounding it to a paste. In 1735 Collinson wrote John Bartram of the hemlock he had received from Roxbury, Massachusetts. (In some of the early references hemlock is called "abies," the present genus of the firs.)

High-bush cranberry—*Viburnum trilobum*

This viburnum, sometimes known as *V. americanum,* is a tall native shrub of northern North America, distinguished by its broadly oval, three-lobed, maplelike leaves, more or less coarsely toothed and oppositely arranged. The flat-topped flower clusters of small white

flowers, margined by much larger sterile flowers, appear on short stalks in May, followed by red fruits. These somewhat resemble the true cranberry, *Vaccinium macrocarpon;* hence the common name. *Viburnum* is the Latin name for the European *V. lantana; trilobum* is descriptive of the leaves of this species, which is closely related to Old World viburnums, including the snowball. In 1736, Peter Collinson asked John Bartram to send him some seeds of "Guelder Rose." Since the sterile snowball, *V. opulus sterile,* was well known to him, here he presumably referred to the high-bush cranberry. All viburnums belong to the honeysuckle family, Caprifoliaceae. (See also snowball.)

Holly—*Ilex opaca*

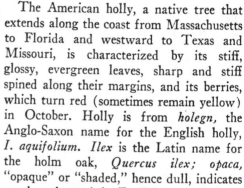

The American holly, a native tree that extends along the coast from Massachusetts to Florida and westward to Texas and Missouri, is characterized by its stiff, glossy, evergreen leaves, sharp and stiff spined along their margins, and its berries, which turn red (sometimes remain yellow) in October. Holly is from *holegn,* the Anglo-Saxon name for the English holly, *I. aquifolium. Ilex* is the Latin name for the holm oak, *Quercus ilex; opaca,* "opaque" or "shaded," hence dull, indicates that the leaves are less glossy than those of the English species. Peter Kalm, who remarked on finding holly in wet places and scattered in the forests of New Jersey, noted that the Swedes there boiled the dried leaves for a pleurisy medicine. Both Washington and Jefferson planted American holly, and Jefferson listed it (but not the English species) as an ornamental. In 1771, he planned a circular burying place, to be surrounded either by untrimmed red cedars or a "stone wall with a holly hedge on it." John Bartram sent berries of the American holly to Peter Collinson. Holly belongs to its own family, Aquifoliaceae, which also includes inkberry, myrtle-leaved holly, winterberry, and yaupon.

Hollyhock—*Althaea rosea*

The word "hollyhock" is medieval English for holy mallow, probably because it was brought from the Holy Land. (A mallow, but not this one, was mentioned by Job.) Through the Latin, *Althaea* comes from the Greek name for the marshmallow, *A. officinalis; rosea* means "rose colored," but the large flowers, which bloom July to September, may be white, red, and sometimes pale yellow, as well as pink. Almost stalkless, they crowd the top of the tall, stout plant stem, facing horizontally. Hollyhocks were cultivated in China for at least a thousand years before they were found by the first Europeans and, in 1573, introduced into England. The American colonists grew red, pink, and white single-flowered varieties very early. Josselyn found them in New England and they were advertised for sale in a Boston newspaper, 1760. John Custis of Williamsburg thanked Peter Collinson in 1735 for his hollyhock seeds, a few of which "came up," and both Jefferson and Lady Skipwith grew them. The hollyhock belongs to the mallow family, Malvaceae. (See also althaea.)

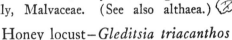

Honey locust—*Gleditsia triacanthos*

The common honey locust, a widely distributed native tree, has large compound, or doubly compound, leaves, the leaflets oval with margins minutely toothed. Stout, usually branched spines several inches long, are characteristic (though the variety *inermis* is thornless). The inconspicuous, greenish flowers appear in short racemes during April and May. The seed pods, a foot long, are flat and more or less twisted. Their sugary pulp, around the seeds, is the source of the common name. Linnaeus named the genus after J. Gottlieb Gleditsch, director of the Berlin botanical garden; *triacanthos* is

Greek for "three-thorned." The honey locust, a member of the great bean family, Leguminosae, was described and illustrated in Catesby's *Natural History,* and there are numerous references to it in colonial times. Peter Collinson, in the *Gentleman's Magazine,* wrote of its importation into England; he had asked Bartram for seeds in 1736. Jefferson twice ordered seeds sent to friends in France. Some white settlers, following Indian practice, used the fruit as food and made beer from the sugary pulp.

Hornbeam—*Carpinus caroliniana*

Hornbeam—also called American hornbeam, blue beech, ironwood, water beech, and hop hornbeam—is a slow-growing tree with very slender, shiny, dark brown twigs. The bark of the older stems is dark gray or blue-gray, smooth and beechlike; the wood beneath is fluted and twisted, suggestive of muscles. The oval-triangular leaves have their teeth subdivided into finer teeth. Oxpoles, which became as hard, or as smooth, as horn, were made from the wood of the

European hornbeam, *C. betulus,* for which *carpinus* was the Latin name. The specific name indicates the general botanical area in which this variety was collected. References are numerous. Catesby mentioned the hornbeam in his *Natural History,* Peter Kalm noted it in Phildaelphia in 1748, and Bartram observed this tree in his travels through the Carolinas, Georgia, and Florida, and on several occasions sent seeds to Peter Collinson. The hornbeam belongs to the birch family, Betulaceae.

Hyacinth—*Hyacinthus orientalis*

Both the common and generic names of this ancient garden plant are from Hyacinthus, the beautiful boy of Greek mythology who was accidentally killed by Apollo, whereupon his blood became a plant, probably this species; the Latin adjective *orientalis* indicates an eastern origin, in this case Asia Minor. The common or Dutch hyacinth, as the plant is also called, is a member of the lily family, Liliaceae, and blooms in March and April. The compact clusters of flowers, pink, blue, lavender, or purple, are borne on a stout green flower stalk 8-18 inches high; each flower, small and bell shaped, is fused into a tube for about half its length, the lobes curling backward. Hyacinths, both single and double, were well known in colonial gardens. John Banister listed them in Virginia in 1688 and a florist of Haarlem, New York, offered bulbs for sale in 1716. Peter Collinson sent John Bartram "Hyacinths, a present from James Gordon, Jr." In 1766, Richard Stockton, future signer of the Declaration of Independence, wrote his wife that she already had "as fine tulips and hyacinths . . . as any in England, yet I shall order some of the finest."

Hydrangea – *Hydrangea aborescens*

This shrub, known also as wild or smooth hydrangea, is native to the eastern United States south of New England. The leaves, opposite, heart shaped to oval, 3-6 inches long, finely saw toothed but usually not at all lobed, are on rather long leafstalks. The white flowers, in June, form large, flat-topped clusters 2-6 inches across. Some marginal flowers may be large and sterile; the fertile flowers, smaller and more numerous, have eight to ten prominently protruding stamens. The common and generic names both come from the Greek *hydor*, "water," and *aggeion*, "vessel," in reference to the cuplike shape of the plant's fruit, a small capsule; *arborescens*, "becoming a tree," is not a very apt description since the wild hydrangea is rarely more than 3 or 4 feet high. This shrub was introduced into England from Virginia in 1736; Collinson wrote in 1746: "My Hydrangea, perhaps the first in England, flowered in . . . my garden at Mill-Hill." The hydrangea is sometimes placed in a small family of its own, Hydrangeaceae, but more often included in the saxifrage family, Saxifragaceae.

Inkberry – *Ilex glabra*

In a letter to Linnaeus, May 18, 1765, Dr. Garden described inkberry as "a very beautiful shrub, about the height of two or three feet." The leathery gray-green leaves, with or without a few dull teeth, are 2 inches long. The small white flowers that bloom in June

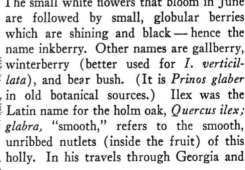

are followed by small, globular berries which are shining and black — hence the name inkberry. Other names are gallberry, winterberry (better used for *I. verticillata*), and bear bush. (It is *Prinos glaber* in old botanical sources.) Ilex was the Latin name for the holm oak, *Quercus ilex; glabra*, "smooth," refers to the smooth, unribbed nutlets (inside the fruit) of this holly. In his travels through Georgia and

Florida in 1765, John Bartram noted "evergreen prinos or ink-berries." A native species ranging from Massachusetts to Florida and westward to Louisiana, inkberry is a member of the holly family, Aquifoliaceae. (See also holly and yaupon.)

Jonquil—*Narcissus jonquilla*

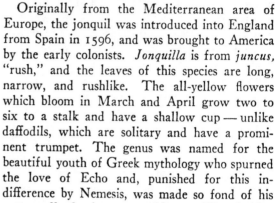

Originally from the Mediterranean area of Europe, the jonquil was introduced into England from Spain in 1596, and was brought to America by the early colonists. *Jonquilla* is from *juncus,* "rush," and the leaves of this species are long, narrow, and rushlike. The all-yellow flowers which bloom in March and April grow two to six to a stalk and have a shallow cup — unlike daffodils, which are solitary and have a prominent trumpet. The genus was named for the beautiful youth of Greek mythology who spurned the love of Echo and, punished for this indifference by Nemesis, was made so fond of his own reflection that eventually he became a flower. The simplex variety of jonquil which grows in the Palace Garden at Williamsburg is believed to be similar to forms known to Jefferson and other colonial gardeners. (See also daffodil.)

Kentucky coffee-tree—*Gymnocladus dioica*

This native tree has large, doubly compound leaves 1-3 feet long, with large, oval, toothless leaflets. The short, heavy, woody pods, pulpy within, are 4-12 inches long and 1-2 inches wide. They hang through the winter, when the stout, thornless twigs have a dead

appearance. The generic name is Greek meaning "naked branches"; *dioica* refers to the dioecious condition of the species, *i.e.,* individual trees may have only staminate or carpellate flowers, not both. The common name derives from the use of the seeds as a substitute for coffee by Kentucky pioneers before and during the Revolution, and later more widely. John Clayton wrote John Bartram, March 16, 1763, "I should, in

particular, be very glad to know if you saw anything of the Canada Bonduc, or Nickar-tree, and if you brought any of the seeds home with you." Jefferson and Washington both planted the tree, which belongs to the Leguminosae, and is sparsely distributed from New York to Tennessee, Minnesota, and Oklahoma.

Larkspur — *Delphinium consolida*

Larkspur, native to England and Europe, is an annual plant that was well known in early American gardens. The garden larkspur has very finely cut, threadlike leaves and clusters of flowers, blue to purple, sometimes white, in June and July. The common name is suggested by the shape of the nectary, a single backward-pointing spur, like the spur of a lark's foot. The generic name is derived from the Latin for the legendary dolphin, and also has reference to the shape of the flower; *consolida,* "solid" or "firm," perhaps describes the dense flower clusters. John Bartram, one of the first to make experiments in hybridization, crossed larkspur types. Peter Collinson commented upon this, in 1760: "I am delighted with his operations on the larkspur. The product's wonderful. If these charming flowers can be continued by seed, they will be the greatest ornament of the garden." Present-day perennial delphiniums are of uncertain hybrid origin; the annual species are derived principally from *D. consolida* or *D. ajacis* — the latter with very large flower clusters. All delphiniums belong to the buttercup family, Ranunculaceae.

Lemon daylily — *Hemerocallis flava*

The Greeks knew the daylily as a flower beautiful for a day, each individual bloom shriveling at the day's end; their words, *hemera,* "day," and *kallos,* "beautiful," are descriptive of this ephemeral quality. *Flava* is the Latin adjective for the color of the flowers which are bright yellow and unspotted as are some species of *Lilium.* They are funnel shaped and bloom in June in small clusters at the top of stiff flower stalks. The leaves, long, narrow or strap shaped, bend over and are smaller than those of the more common tawny daylily, *H. fulva,* which blooms a week or so earlier than the lemon

species. The lemon daylily was introduced into England in 1596 from "Siberia" where the Tartars used the leaves to make saddle mats. According to *Gardens of Colony and State,* the lemon daylily was known in the American colonies before 1700. Walter lists it as "sea daffodil" in his *Flora Caroliniana;* Lady Skipwith's garden records include both the "Yellow and Tawny Day Lilys," members of the lily family, Liliaceae.

Lilac—*Syringa vulgaris*

The common lilac has been cultivated in Europe since 1554; Busbequius, Austrian ambassador to Constantinople, is credited with bringing it to Vienna from southeastern Europe. It was introduced into England in 1597, and into America, according to one record, in 1652. Collinson, sending lilacs to John Bartram in 1737, wrote "Colonel Custis at Williamsburg . . . has undoubtedly the best collection in that country." Washington, Jefferson, and Lady Skipwith planted lilacs and both blue and white varieties are listed in Prince's catalogue. Lilac has opposite leaves, broad-ovate, 2-6 inches long, heart shaped or straight at the base. The dense flower clusters, about 6 inches long, which bloom in April and May, are usually "lilac," sometimes purplish or white. Lilac is from *lilag* or *lilaj,* the Persian name for this shrub or for "flower," the ultimate root meaning "bluish." The generic name, probably from the Greek *syrinx,* "a pipe," was originally applied to *Philadelphus,* or mock orange — still popularly called syringa — and transferred to lilac. The specific name means "common" in the sense of well known, abundant. Lilac belongs to the olive family, Oleaceae.

Lily of the valley—*Convallaria majalis*

Lily of the valley is prized for the fragrance of the small, white, bell-shaped flowers which dangle in a one-sided row from a flower stalk that rises between two large, shiny leaves, unusually broad for

a member of the lily family, Liliaceae.
Blooming in April or May, it is also known
as May lily; in England its local folk names
include lily confancy and mugget. It is the
"lilly conually" mentioned in the very early
garden book, *Maison Rustique,* 1616, and
the "Convallaria majalis of the Cherokees"
that charmed William Bartram. Jefferson
planted it at Monticello and Lady Skipwith
had "Lily of the Valley" in her garden,
probably purchased from Minton Collins of Richmond. The generic
name, *Convallaria,* is from the Latin for valley; *majalis* is from
maius, "May," and signifies May-flowering. This species apparently
is native both to Europe and to the Appalachians of America and is
thus a good example of scattered, world-wide distribution.

Live oak—*Quercus virginiana*

The live oak, a native tree that ranges southward from Virginia
along the coast to Mexico, has large, spreading, almost horizontal
limbs; the crown is sometimes twice as broad as the tree is tall. The
stiff, oblong, evergreen leaves, 2-4 inches long and occasionally
toothed, are dark green above and white felty beneath. The common
name was coined in Virginia at least as early as 1610, "live" because
evergreen, "oak" from the Anglo-Saxon name, *ac,* for the English
oak. The generic name is from the Latin for an oak tree; *virginiana*
refers to the southern botanical region. According to Mark Catesby,
the Indians ground acorns of this oak "to thicken their venison-soop"
and also ate them with hominy and wild rice. The wood of the live
oak is perhaps the heaviest, and hardest, of all the oaks. From scores

 of early references it is known the wood
was used for wagons, tool handles, and ship
construction. In the days of wooden ships
the United States Navy owned large
reservations of live-oak timberland in
Georgia, Florida, and Louisiana. Just as
the British Navy once depended on the
English oak, so did the ships of the line of
our fleet depend upon the native live oak,
a member of the beech family, Fagaceae.

Lizard's-tail – *Saururus cernuus*

Lizard's-tail is a swamp plant indigenous to the eastern United States. Conspicuous from June to August, the very small, creamy white flowers form a dense, tapering spike, drooping at its tip, that somewhat resembles a lizard's tail. The leaves are heart shaped and pointed, on a crooked, conspicuously jointed stem. This member of the pepper family, Piperaceae, is not out of place in a naturalistic garden. The generic name is compounded from the Greek words *sauros,* "lizard," and *oura,* "tail"; the specific name, *cernuus,* means "bending" or "bowing." The lizard's-tail was introduced into England from "Virginia" in 1759. John Bartram noted it in Florida, and an "Aristolochia" root Collinson asked him to get may have been this species. Cadwallader Colden, Lieutenant Governor of New York and a botanist, received "seeds of saururus" from Bartram in 1745.

Loblolly pine – *Pinus taeda*

The native evergreen tree, loblolly pine, bears bundles of three coarse needles, 6-9 inches long. The staminate cone clusters are prominent in May. (The Virginia scrub pine, *P. virginiana,* has two, shorter needles to a bundle.) Loblolly is of uncertain application but possibly comes from the American dialect term for a mudpuddle. Old field pine and frankincense pine are other names sometimes used. *Pinus,* the old Latin name for pine, is from the Greek *pinos,* also the pine; the Latin *taeda* connotes "resinous, suitable for torches." Michaux noted that three-fourths of the houses in Virginia were built of loblolly pine, which provides better timber than scrub pine. Pine was frequently specified for construction. It was designated for the flooring of the Capitol in Williamsburg in 1700. Jefferson listed "Black or pitch pine, Pinus taeda" as "useful for fabrication." Loblolly pine

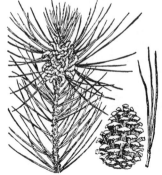

was introduced into England in 1713. This member of the pine family, Pinaceae, ranges from Delaware to Texas along the coast. (See also white pine.)

Locust—*Robinia pseudo-acacia*

The locust tree, also called black, common, and yellow locust, and false acacia, has compound leaves with seven to twenty-one leaflets. At the base of each leaf are two short, divergent thorns — modified stipules. Drooping clusters of white, beanlike flowers appear in May or June, followed by seed pods 3-4 inches long. Locust is from the Latin *locusta,* "grasshopper" or "locust," but the application is obscure. The genus was named for Jean Robin, herbalist to Henry IV of France, and his son Vespasian. A native tree ranging from Pennsylvania to Georgia and westward to Missouri, the locust was introduced into England in 1640 and is now widely grown in Europe. When Philadelphia was laid out in 1683, a principal street was named for this tree. Virginia colonists used the wood for posts and ground sills. Captain William Fitzhugh of Bedford, Virginia, enclosed his orchard with locust fencing which, according to a letter he wrote in 1686, was "as durable as most brick walls."

Love-lies-bleeding—*Amaranthus caudatus*

This annual herb with a fanciful common name grows up to 3 feet in height and blooms in June or later, depending on the time

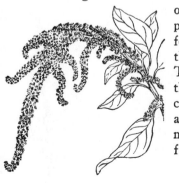

of sowing. The minute, scaly flowers, red-purple, sometimes scarlet or yellowish, form slender, drooping, tassellike spikes, the terminal one longest and most taillike. The generic name is from Greek words that mean "unfading," in reference to the calyx and bracts which do not wither for a long time; *caudatus,* from the Latin, means "tailed." Introduced into England from the East Indies in 1596, love-lies-bleeding was grown in Gerard's garden the same year. This relative of the cockscomb was advertised for sale in Boston in 1760. It is a member of the amaranth family, Amaranthaceae — one of the few of that group worthy of cultivation in a garden.

Magnolia — *Magnolia grandiflora*

"The Magnolia is the finest and most superb ever-green tree that the earth produced," wrote Dr. Alexander Garden to Charles Whitworth in 1757. He was but one of many early writers to appreciate the southern magnolia, or bull bay—a native species ranging from North Carolina to Texas. The large, oblong, shiny, evergreen leaves, stiff, leathery, and rusty-wooly on the lower surface; the large white, cup-shaped flowers — 6-8 inches across, solitary at the ends of rusty-wooly twigs; and the fruit, a rusty-wooly cone with red seeds that become visible upon ripening— all are characteristic. The genus was named for Pierre Magnol (1638-1715), a professor of medicine and director of the botanic gardens, Montpelier, France; *grandiflora* means "large flowers." Introduced into England "from Carolina" in 1734, this member of the magnolia family, Magnoliaceae, was referred to as "M. altissima, the Laurel Tree of Carolina," by Catesby in his *Natural History*. Individual references to this handsome "great magnolia" in colonial times are many and it was widely planted ornamentally.

Meadow rue — *Thalictrum minus adiantifolium*

Meadow rue, or maid-of-the-mist, blooms in June. The loose, filmy clusters of yellow-green flowers with very narrow "petals" (really sepals) and many conspicuous stamens give the plant a delicate, lacy appearance. The leaves resemble those of a maidenhair fern. The generic name is the Latin noun for meadow rue, derived from the older Greek name given by Dioscorides to a plant the identity of which is uncertain; *minus* means

"smaller," and the varietal name means "leaves like an adiantum," or maidenhair fern. Meadow rue, native to England, Europe, Asia, and North Africa, is a member of the rather primitive buttercup family, Ranunculaceae. (The true rue is *Ruta* of the orange family.) Kalm noted, on May 1, 1649, at Raccoon, New Jersey "The Thalictra or Meadow-Rue had both their flowers and leaves hurt by frost."

Mimosa—*Albizzia julibrissin*

The white-streaked, greenish twigs and the doubly compound leaves, with their very small leaflets arranged like parts of a feather and appearing late, are characteristic of the mimosa or silk tree, an introduced species from Persia and central China. The threadlike flowers, borne in pink tufts, appear in June and July and are succeeded by flat pods, 4-5 inches long by ½ inch wide, that show the outlines of the seeds within. This medium-sized tree reached England "from the Levant" in 1745 as "Acacia julibrissin." Its introduction into South Carolina at the end of the eighteenth century is attributed to André Michaux. Mimosa is from the recent Latin *mimos,* "mimic," and was the name given to the true mimosa, *Mimosa pudica,* a related herb with sensitive leaves. The genus was named for Albizzi, a well-born Italian naturalist who is said to have introduced the species into Italy; *julibrissin* is a Persian local name. Mimosa is not hardy much farther north than Washington, D.C., but is a common escape in the southern states. It belongs to the large bean family, Leguminosae.

Mock orange—*Philadelphus coronarius*

The mock orange, or sweet syringa, is not, of course, a true orange although the scent of some forms suggests orange blossoms. It is a shrub with broad, oval, abruptly pointed, and minutely toothed opposite leaves, 1½-4 inches long. The creamy white flowers of moderate size bloom in May or June in terminal clusters of five to seven, and usually are very fragrant (some varieties and related species are odorless). The generic name was transferred by Linnaeus from another plant named after Ptolemy Philadelphus, King of Egypt

(285-247 B.C.), who held his banquets amidst lavish gardens; *coronarius* implies "suitable for garlands or wreaths." In 1596 mock orange was introduced into England. It was mentioned by William Bartram as "Philadelphus," listed as "syringa" by Prince, and referred to as "Syringa or Mock Orange" by Lady Skipwith. A member of the saxifrage family, Saxifragaceae, the mock orange's natural range is from Italy to the Caucasus.

Moneywort—*Lysimachia nummularia*

Moneywort gets its name from its coin-shaped leaves; in its native England other local names include creeping Charlie, creeping Jane or Jenny, and herb twopence. A very low, running plant, it has round, opposite leaves. The small yellow flowers bloom in May and June in the axils of the leaves. *Lysimachia,* from a Latin plant name, comes ultimately from the Greek, in honor of King Lysimachus of Thrace; *nummularia* means "little coins." A plant so readily propagated and native to England reasonably can be assumed to have crossed the Atlantic at an early date. Peter Collinson wrote John Bartram, May 2, 1738, "It is a great advantage to send plants with a sod of earth about them; for many times there comes up odd plants — as it happened this year . . . in the rods of Herb Twopence." Moneywort belongs to the primrose family, Primulaceae.

Mountain laurel—*Kalmia latifolia*

The mountain laurel, a native shrub of eastern North America, has evergreen leaves, 3-4 inches long, dark green above, yellow-green beneath, that grow in whorls or clusters at the ends of the twigs. It is best recognized by its large terminal clusters of shallow, bowl-shaped flowers, white or pink with small purple markings. These bloom in May and, before pollination, the ten stamens are held in pockets near the rim of the corolla. This member of the heath family, Ericaceae, is neither restricted to mountainous regions nor related to the true laurel, *Laurus nobilis*. The genus was named by Linnaeus for his pupil, Peter Kalm, who traveled in America 1748-51; *latifolia* means "broad leaves." Common names include American laurel and calico bush—the spotted flowers suggesting calico prints. Kalm reported that it was called spoonwood by Swedish colonists because the Indians made spoons from the wood of plants sufficiently large for this purpose. There are numerous other records in colonial times. Though Mark Catesby tried also, Peter Collinson first successfully introduced mountain laurel into England in 1734 and had it blooming by 1740. Jefferson wrote John Bartram the Younger for plants to send to France.

Myrtle-leaved holly—*Ilex myrtifolia*

This southern shrub bears distinctive, evergreen leaves, 1-2 inches long, that are very narrow and relatively thick. They are stiff, with an abrupt point at the tip that often is bent downward; the margin of each leaf may or may not have a few short teeth near the tip.

The clustered berries are bright red, as are those of most hollies. *Ilex* was the Latin name for the holm oak, *Quercus ilex;* the specific name, *myrtifolia,* means "leaves like the myrtle." In a number of botanical references this species is given as variety *myrtifolia* of the closely related dahoon, *Ilex cassine* L., but present authorities regard it as a species in its own right. It was mentioned in William Bartram's *Travels* as "Ilex myrtifolium." Apparently the myrtle-leaved holly was not introduced into England until 1806, and then from the West Indies. The natural range of this plant, a member of the holly family, Aquifoliaceae, is from North Carolina to Florida.

Nasturtium—*Tropaeolum majus*

This garden annual of the nasturtium family, Tropaeolaceae, has a distinctive round leaf, with the leafstalk attached below, at the

center. The flowers, 2½ inches wide, trumpet shaped and long spurred, bloom in midsummer in shades of yellow and orange, often marked with red. *Nasturtium* was the Latin name for some pungent cress, compounded from *nasus,* "nose," and *torquere,* "to twist" or "to torture," hence to affect the sense of smell. The generic name apparently is from the Greek *tropaion,* "trophy," in reference to the shield-shaped leaves and the helmet-shaped flowers; the Latin *majus,* "larger," is in contrast to the dwarf nasturtium, *T. minus.* One record gives 1686 as the date of the nasturtium's introduction into England from Peru; another source indicates that Gerard grew *T. majus* before 1596. John Randolph of Williamsburg noted in his *Treatise on Gardening* (*c.* 1765-70), that "It is thought the flower is superior to a radish in flavour, and is eat in salads, or *without.*" Thomas Jefferson planted "Nasturtium in 35 little hills" at Monticello.

Oriental poppy—*Papaver orientale*

The Oriental poppy is recognized by its large, orange-red, shallow-cupped flowers, with five or six petals and purplish-black centers. They bloom during April and May, each flower solitary on a thick hairy stalk growing to a height of 2-3 feet; the stiff leaves also are conspicuously hairy. The word "poppy" is a variant of the Anglo-Saxon cognate of *papaver* — Latin name for the poppy and now for the genus — the ultimate meaning of which is obscure; *orientale,* "eastern," refers to the place of  origin, Asia Minor. The Oriental poppy, a member of the poppy family, Papaveraceae, was introduced into England from Armenia in 1714. In 1741, Peter Collinson sent seeds to John Bartram. This poppy was advertised for sale in Boston in 1760. Jefferson several times mentioned the "larger Poppy" and the "Lesser poppy," and in 1771 planned to have the poppy as a "hardy perennial flower" for his garden at Monticello.

Osage orange—*Maclura pomifera*

The Osage orange is a deciduous tree indigenous to Missouri, Oklahoma, Arkansas, and Texas — the Osage country. The large, green, orangelike fruits are distinctive, as are the stout spines scattered along the branches. The leaves are broadly triangular, without lobes or teeth. The genus was named for William Maclure (1763-1840), a Scottish geologist who made his home in America; *pomifera* means "fruit-bearing." Osage orange, a member of the mulberry family, Moraceae, is also called bowwood and bois d'Arc (the Indians made bows and clubs of the tough, strong wood), Osage apple tree, and hedgetree (the colonists used it as a natural hedge plant). From the wood the Indians also extracted an orange dye and the base for a green dye. It is believed that the plant was used for cattle enclosures in Virginia in colonial times.

Pansy—*Viola tricolor hortensis*

The pansy, familiar in gardens and in the pages of English literature, is one of the oldest of cultivated flowers. Its large velvety petals—in size out of proportion to the small, toothed leaves — are blue, purple, yellow, white, deep purplish-red, or in three-colored combinations. The word "pansy" is from the French *pensée,* "thought" or "remembrance." *Viola* was the Latin name for violet; *tricolor* means "three-colored"; *hortensis,* "pertaining to gardens." The pansy, European in origin and a member of the violet family, Violaceae, was developed before the eighteenth century from the wild pansy with small purple and yellow flowers which the colonists called Johnny-jump-up. Among scores of English common names are heartsease, love-in-idleness, herb trinity, and—the longest common name ever given to a plant — meet-her-in-the-entry-and-kiss-her-in-the-buttery. John Lawson mentioned "Tres

Colores"; pansies were advertised in Boston in 1760, and Jefferson sowed "tricolor" in 1767. (See also violet.)

Paper mulberry—*Broussonetia papyrifera*

This tree, a member of the mulberry family, Moraceae, has triangular or heart-shaped, pointed leaves, coarsely toothed, rough above and velvety-hairy beneath. Especially in older trees, some leaves are mitten shaped, like those of the sassafras; others may be lobed, like fig leaves. The trunks of older trees are curiously gnarled and twisted. The genus is named for Broussonet, a French physician and naturalist of Montpelier (1761-1807); the specific name refers to the use of the inner bark in producing paper, from which, for centuries, paper lanterns and umbrellas have been made in Japan. Until several generations ago this species, originating in China, Japan, and the East Indies, provided tapa cloth, the chief clothing of Polynesians. The paper mulberry—introduced into England from China by Collinson in 1751 and grown in this country by Thomas Jefferson — should not be confused with mulberries of the genus *Morus.* The Virginia colonists attempted to make use of the native red mulberry, *M. rubra,* in starting a silk industry; when the silkworms refused to eat the leaves, the white mulberry, *M. alba,* was imported from China in 1621. The industry failed, nevertheless, for want of cheap labor.

Peony—*Paeonia officinalis*

"If new brought from *America,* the whole Botanic World would resound with its praise" wrote John Hill in his *Eden,* 1757, lamenting the neglect of the peony by English gardeners. A herbaceous perennial, flowering in April or May, this peony has large pink to dark red flower heads, one to a stalk, 3-4 inches across, with large, often numerous petals; the leaves are much cut, sometimes twice compound. Both the

common and generic names are from the Latin, derived in turn from the Greek name for this plant which was called after Paeon, the physician-god of healing, because of its supposed medicinal qualities. The specific name is a Latin adjective with similar connotations. This member of the buttercup family, Ranunculaceae, was introduced into cultivation in England from Europe in 1548. Jefferson planned to have "piony" in his garden at Monticello, according to his Account Book.

Periwinkle—*Vinca minor*

Periwinkle is a ground-covering, mat-forming plant with opposite leaves about 1½ inches long, narrowly oval, thickish, stiff, evergreen, and shiny. The flowers are pale blue or lavender, sometimes white, about an inch across; they have a short corolla tube which flares into five separate petals. Periwinkle, variously spelled "pervenke," "pervinke," "parvenk," and "parwynke" by Chaucer and his contemporaries, comes from the old Latin name for this genus, *pervinca* or *vinca*. The ultimate meaning is uncertain, but *vinca* perhaps comes from *vincere*, "to conquer," and suggests the crowding out of other plants; *minor*, "smaller," distinguishes this species from *V. major*, with larger leaves and flowers, reddish-lavender to blue. *V. minor* has been so long cultivated in England that it is considered native there, but it is from the continent. Pliny mentions its cultivation in Rome in the first century. In 1771 Jefferson included this member of the dogbane family, Apocynaceae, in his plans for the improvement of his garden at Monticello.

Persian lilac—*Syringa persica*

Persian lilac is a shrub in the olive family, Oleaceae, with opposite leaves, narrowly ovate, 1½-3 inches long, more or less tapered at the base, on slender arching stems. The loose clusters of pale lilac flowers which bloom in April or May are 3-4 inches long. (The common lilac has larger leaves and flower clusters and a stiffer stem.) The Persian name of this plant was *lilag* or *lilaj*, hence "lilac." Syringa is probably from the Greek *syrinx*, "a pipe" (for explanation

of this application, see lilac). As the specific name implies, Persian lilac was introduced into England from Persia, which, with Afghanistan and near-by China, is its original home. Miller's *Figures of Plants* puts the date at about 1631, but most authorities, including Paxton, give it as 1640. Lady Skipwith had "Persian Lilacs" as well as the more common types in her garden at Prestwould in Virginia.

Persimmon—*Diospyros virginiana*

The persimmon tree is best recognized by the bark, which has rectangular plates like an alligator's skin, and by the soft, plumlike, red-orange fruits, edible but astringent with tannins until fully ripe. The common name is a variant of *pessimin,* or *putchamin,* the Virginia Indian name. The genus, compounded from the Greek *dios,* "divine," and *pyron,* "grain," is an extravagant allusion to the fruit; the specific name indicates the general botanical area where this member of the ebony family, Ebenaceae, native to eastern North America, was first collected. De Soto ate persimmons in 1557 and references in colonial times are very numerous. Although an early traveler in Pennsylvania wrote: "The pessamins [were] harsh and choakie and furre in a man's mouth, like allam," opinions were generally favorable. The fruits, recently found to have a high vitamin C content, were eaten raw or made into persimmon beer. The plant was introduced into England in 1629.

Pickerel-weed—*Pontederia cordata*

An aquatic plant native to eastern North America, pickerel-weed grows in shallow water at the margins of lakes that may or may not contain pickerel! Alligator wampee is another common name sometimes used. The short-lived, light violet-blue flowers come in June, in a tall spike; each flower is more or less funnel shaped, two lipped, and notched at the base like an arrowhead. This species was introduced into cultivation in England from North America in 1759, according to one record, but Peter Collinson wrote: "Received from J. Bartram, January 17, 1751, a root of Pontedera." The genus was named for Giulio Pontedera, an Italian botanist and professor at Padua, *c.* 1730; the specific name, from the Latin for "heart," refers to the heart-shaped leaf, which has a deep cleft in the base. This plant, which belongs to the pickerel-weed family, Pontederiaceae, was often noted by John Bartram in his travels in Florida, and also observed by Peter Kalm near Montreal in 1749.

Pink locust—*Robinia hispida*

"It has been so loaded with flowers, I am obliged to prop up the branches. It is the glory of our garden and flowers twice a year." Thus, in 1767, did Peter Collinson describe the "Red Acacia" which John Bartram had sent him. Earlier, in 1755, he had written

Linnaeus that a pink locust received from J. Lambol of South Carolina had flowered for the first time. Unlike the common locust, the pink locust of southern gardens is a low shrub. The much-divided leaves have seven to thirteen small, round leaflets, about 1 inch long. In May and June the few-flowered, drooping clusters of rose-pink, beanlike flowers appear. The fruit, a bristly pod 2-3 inches long, rarely develops. The genus, which includes the locust described on page 57, was named for Jean Robin; the specific name means "bristly," "coarsely hairy." The pink locust, or rose acacia as it is sometimes called, ranges from Virginia to Alabama and belongs to the large bean family, Leguminosae.

Pinkster—*Rhododendron nudiflorum*

Pinkster, pink azalea, or wild honeysuckle (sometimes identified as *Azalea nudiflora*), is a native shrub, usually under 5 feet. The conspicuous clusters of six to twelve pink to nearly white flowers, with light red much-protruding stamens, bloom in April and May

67

before the leaves appear; each flower is tubular, somewhat two lipped, and five lobed at the end. Though in no other way related, the pinkster shares with the grass pink the derivation of its common name from the German word *Pingster,* "Pentecost." The Dutch colonial name was *pingsterbloem,* "flower of Pingster," and in the seventeenth century the Dutch of Nieuw Amsterdam gathered the flowers during their Whitsunday festivals. *Rhododendron,* Greek for "rose tree," was originally applied to an oleander; *nudiflorum* is Latin for "naked flower," in reference to the appearance of the flowers before the leaves. Collinson is credited with the introduction of this member of the heath family, Ericaceae, into England in 1734. Kalm, who saw them in New Jersey, wrote "the beauty of the colour entitles them to a place in every flower garden." Early in the eighteenth century crosses between this species and flame azalea, *R. calendulaceum,* with strains of the Asiatic species, *R. luteum,* resulted in the Ghent azaleas. In *Notes on the State of Virginia,* Jefferson refers to the pinkster as "Upright honeysuckle. Azalea nudiflora" which makes it clear he meant this species and not *Lonicera,* true honeysuckle.

Poet's narcissus—*Narcissus poeticus*

Poet's narcissus, blooming in April, is identified by its white perianth with a shallow yellow cup, the margin of which is commonly red or gold. The flowers are solitary. (In contrast, the daffodil has a large central trumpet, as long as or longer than the segments of the perianth; the jonquil has several all-yellow flowers to a stalk.) The leaves are flat and bladelike. Poet's narcissus, a member of the amaryllis family, Amaryllidaceae, was introduced into America from Europe where it was long cultivated.

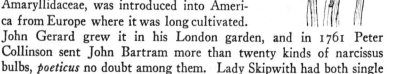

John Gerard grew it in his London garden, and in 1761 Peter Collinson sent John Bartram more than twenty kinds of narcissus bulbs, *poeticus* no doubt among them. Lady Skipwith had both single and double narcissi at Prestwould. For the origin of the generic name see jonquil. The common name may very possibly have been inspired by the whiteness or the fragrance of the flowers.

Red bay—*Persea pubescens*

Red bay, or smooth bay, is an evergreen tree native in swamps from Virginia to Florida. The light green and conspicuously veined leaves, with rusty-brown leafstalks, are long-oval and tapered at each end. The blue-black fruits are borne on red stalks, hence red bay. Bay is from the French *baie* and the Latin *baca,* and connotes the tree's resemblance to the true bay or laurel, *Laurus nobilis.* The generic name is derived through the Latin from the Greek term for some ancient Persian or Egyptian tree with sweet fruit; *pubescens* is Latin, meaning "covered with fine soft hairs." Bay trees — either this species, or the closely related *P. borbonia,* both belonging to the laurel family, Lauraceae—were noted when the Dividing Line between Virginia and North Carolina was run in 1711. William Bartram frequently mentioned "redbay" in his *Travels,* but made no distinction between the two species. John Bartram's diary mentions that the wood of the red bay was used for "A very handsome stair case." Dr. Garden sent "Red Bay" to Ellis in 1755, and Jefferson listed it as an ornamental in his *Notes on the State of Virginia.*

Red buckeye—*Aesculus pavia*

Red buckeye or dwarf flowering chestnut is a native shrub or small crooked tree that ranges from the southeastern part of Virginia to Florida and Louisiana. The opposite compound leaves have five leaflets, broadest near the tip and pointed like those of other members of the horse-chestnut family, Hippocastanaceae. Large, loose clusters of bright red to purplish-red flowers are borne in April or May. "Buckeye"refers to the shape,

69

size, and color of the nuts of some horse chestnuts. *Aesculus* was the Latin name for an oak species and was transferred by Linneaus; *pavia* is an old generic name for horse chestnuts that honors Peter Pav, a Dutch botanist, at one time a professor at the University of Leyden. In colonial times in the Carolinas the soapy mucilage from the bark and roots was used for washing clothes. Frequently mentioned by the early botanists and first sent to England in 1711, this plant was described and illustrated in Catesby's *Natural History* and listed by John Bartram as "Aesculus Caroliniana—Scarlet flowering Horse Chestnut." Jefferson sent this species from Philadelphia in 1798 to be planted at Monticello.

Redbud—*Cercis canadensis*

In March or April, before the heart-shaped leaves unfold, pink to red-purple flowers appear upon the dark branches of the redbud. The fruit of this small native tree is a thin leathery pod, about 3 inches long. *Cercis* is the ancient Greek name for the European redbud; the specific name indicates the general botanical area north of Virginia from which it was first collected—the redbud ranges from Ontario and New York to Florida and westward to Texas. Another common name is Judas tree because the closely similar European *C. siliquastrum* was one of the species thought to be the tree on which Judas Iscariot hanged himself. This member of the large bean family, Leguminosae, was noted by many early travelers and reached England in 1730. Catesby illustrated it in his *Natural History* and Peter Kalm, in Philadelphia, wrote in 1749 of "cercis Canadensis, the Sallod tree." The flowers were occasionally eaten in salads, and the buds pickled by the French in Canada.

Red cedar—*Juniperus virginiana*

This native evergreen tree with reddish scaly bark is a member of the pine family, Pinaceae. It is in fact a juniper (the true cedar is *Cedrus*). There are two kinds of leaves: minute, prickly needles (juvenile foliage), and minute, opposite-appearing scales (adult

foliage). The soft, globular, bluish, berry-like structures are the ovulate cones. The generic name is the old Latin for junipers; the specific name indicates the area in which it was first collected. Early references are almost beyond count. Long before Jefferson listed it as "useful for fabrication" it was prized for the durable quality of its aromatic wood, especially for fences and posts. From at least 1660 on, wills itemized cedar furniture. In 1699, plans for the "Capitole, now erecting in the City of Williamsburg" were revised to specify that the porches stand on cedar columns. Ships approaching the coast in the first period of colonization often were greeted by the pungent smoke of red cedars burning—with other trees—in fires set by the Indians to head game. John Bartram wrote "Col. Byrd is very prodigalle . . . in new Gates, gravel walk hedges and cedars finely turned . . . in short he hath the finest seat in Virginia." Red cedar was sent to England from North America in 1664.

Red chokeberry—*Aronia arbutifolia*

Chokeberry is so called because of the astringent quality of the fruits, which resemble very small red apples. The generic name is derived from *aria,* an ancient name for the whitebeam tree, *Sorbus aria; arbutifolia* refers to the arbutuslike leaves (the comparison is with plants of the genus *Arbutus* and not the trailing arbutus, *Epigaea repens*). This shrub, a native of the eastern United States and a member of the rose family, Rosaceae, has oblong leaves, 1½-3 inches long, with small, dark glands along the midrib on the upper surface. Terminal clusters of white, cherry-like flowers, with black anthers, bloom in April or May. The fruits, conspicuous in September and October, are said to have been cooked by the Indians to make a heavy, sweet, dark red jelly. The red chokeberry was introduced into cultivation in England as "Pyrus arbutifolia" in 1700, and will be found under that name in some references. Thomas Jefferson called his *Aronia* "choak cherries."

Rose mallow—*Hibiscus moscheutos*

Rose mallow is a wild perennial herb found, typically, in brackish, but also in fresh-water marshes from Massachusetts to Florida. In July and August, the plant bears a few pink or creamy white, five-petaled flowers, 4-7 inches across, on stalks that grow from the bases of the upper leaves. Typical leaves are oval, 3-7 inches long, and more or less white-felty beneath. Other common names include swamp mallow, sea hollyhock, and marshmallow (better applied to the related true marshmallow, *Althaea officinalis*). *Hibiscus* is the old Latin name for a mallow; *moscheutos* is also a pre-Linnaean term for some kind of mallow. Lady Skipwith had a "Crimson Mallow" in her garden and Jefferson wrote, on July 5, 1767, "Eastern Mallow almost vanished [from bloom], an indifferent flower." On July 18, however, it was again "in bloom." The date of introduction into England is uncertain. All mallows belong to the mallow family, Malvaceae.

St.-John's-wort—*Hypericum calycinum*

St.-John's-wort is an evergreen, more or less prostrate garden plant, but with some erect stems. The leaves are opposite, 3-4 inches long; the proportionately large flowers, one to a stem, which bloom in July and August, have very many stamens. In England *H. perforatum* was believed to have the power of warding off evil spirits, especially on the eve of St. John, June 23; hence the common name St.-John's-wort which was extended to other species of the genus. *Hypericum,* from *hypo,* "under," and *erica,* "heather," was an old Greek name for some unknown plant that may have grown "under the heather"; the specific name, "like a calyx," is obscure. Among a number of British folk names occasionally used are Aaron's beard and rose of Sharon (the latter better used for the althaea, *Hibiscus syriacus*). Considered native in Ire-

72

land, but an introduced species from southeastern Europe and Asia Minor, St.-John's-wort has been cultivated in the British Isles since 1676. All species of *Hypericum,* including the American *H. prolificum,* or shrubby St.-John's-wort in the Palace Garden, belong to the St.-John's-wort family, Hypericaceae.

Scarlet oak—*Quercus coccinea*

This deciduous tree, belonging to the beech or oak family, Fagaceae, has glossy green leaves deeply cut, each lobe sharply toothed, and each tooth bristle tipped — typical of all red or black oaks. (Broad-leaved oaks without bristles belong to the white oak group.) The leaves turn bright red in the fall. "Oak" comes from the Anglo-Saxon *ac,* the name for the English oak, *Q. robur.* The generic name *Quercus,* selected by Linnaeus, was the Latin common name for the oak tree; *coccinea* means "scarlet." A native species ranging from Maine to Florida and far westward, the scarlet oak is particularly common in the mountains and Piedmont of the south, and was usually included in the plant records of the colonial period. It was repeatedly noted by John Bartram in his travels in the southeastern colonies, and was introduced into England in 1691. In 1745, Launcelot Lee of England wrote Thomas Lee of Virginia asking for seeds of several trees, including the "scarlet oak." (See also live oak, white oak.)

Scotch broom—*Cytisus scoparius*

In late April and May this shrub, with bright green, four-sided stems and small leaflets, bears a profusion of beanlike, but vivid yellow flowers along the stems and at the top. The fruit is a pod 1-2 inches long. Scotch broom is native in all the British Isles and Europe as well as Scotland. The stems once were used for brooms in parts of England. *Cytisus* comes from the Greek *kytisos,* the name of some cloverlike plant with three leaflets; the specific name is from the Latin *scopa,* "a broom." In a letter of December 20, 1736, Peter Collinson asked John Bartram "Pray does English broom grow?" Dr. J. M. Galt of Williamsburg is credited with introducing Scotch broom into Virginia; while a medical student abroad in 1765-67 he collected seed which he sent to John H. Cocke of Mount Pleasant, recommending broom as summer feed for "sheep & Hogs." This member of the bean family, Leguminosae, is now naturalized along the Atlantic coast.

Scotch rose—*Rosa spinosissima*

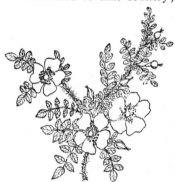

This rose has been grown in Scotland for centuries but is not restricted to that country; it ranges from western Europe eastward to China. *Rosa* is the Latin name for a rose; the specific name means "most prickly" — the stems are very densely bristled and also have straight, scattered thorns. Another common name is burnet rose, derived from the superficial resemblance of the leaves to salad burnet, *Sanguisorba minor*. Sometimes there are five, but usually seven to nine, even eleven, small leaflets, ½-¾ inches long. The pink, white, or yellowish flowers, solitary, but usually very numerous along the branches, bloom in June and later. Gerard referred to this species as "rose-bearing apples." Scotch rose, a member of the rose family, Rosaceae, was generally included in old-fashioned rose gardens.

Shadbush—*Amelanchier canadensis*

A shrub or small tree with smooth, gray bark, shadbush is native to eastern North America; from Nova Scotia to Florida it blooms at the time the shad run up the rivers to spawn — in Virginia, March or April. White, narrow-petaled flowers are produced abundantly before the leaves, which resemble those of the apple, have fully developed. Young leaves are white-downy and some soft hairs persist on both sides. The edible but rather tasteless fruits, red-purple and apple shaped, were esteemed by the Indians and eaten by explorers, raw or in pies and muffins—hence the name serviceberry or "sarviceberry." Other common names are Juneberry, shadblow, and May cherry. The genus is from a Savoy name for the medlar, *Mespilus germanica.* The specific name refers to the general botanical region north of Virginia. Peter Collinson asked John Bartram in 1736 for seeds of "Services"; Walter referred to "Mespilus amelanchier" in his *Flora Caroliniana.* Shadbush belongs to the rose family, Rosaceae.

Siberian squill—*Scilla sibirica*

Siberian squill is a March-flowering bulbous plant 4-6 inches high. Usually there are several flower stalks which bear one to five deep blue, shallowly bell-shaped flowers, with each lobe flaring. The leaves are about ¼ inch wide. The old Greek name for this group of plants— which includes the bell-flowered squill — was *scilla,* from *skyllein,* "to injure," because the bulbs of some species are poisonous. The common name derives from the Latin form, *squilla,* the French *squille.* The specific name refers to Siberia, the country of origin. The Siberian squill, a member of the lily family, Liliaceae, was introduced into England in 1796, and bulbs probably were sent to America soon after.

Silver-bell tree—*Halesia carolina*

In April and May this diminutive native tree bears small, white, bell-shaped flowers, each about ¾ inches long, that hang profusely along the branches in clusters of two to five. The leaves, which resemble those of the cherry, are alternate, short stalked, and finely blunt toothed. The oblong, four-winged fruits, green at first, turn a light brown. The genus was named in honor of Stephen Hales (1677-1761), an English botanist and inventor, author of *Vegetable Staticks;* the specific name refers to the area where the plant was first found. Silver-bell tree, also called snowdrop tree, was illustrated in Catesby's *Natural History* and named "H. tetraptera." It was introduced into England in 1756, apparently first by John Clayton of Virginia. John Ellis also received seeds from Dr. Garden about this time. In 1766, Peter Collinson wrote John Bartram on the flora of the Carolinas, and included the "Halesias." This species, with a natural range from the mountains of West Virginia to Florida and westward to Illinois and Texas, belongs to the storax family, Styracaceae.

Snowball—*Viburnum opulus sterile*

Snowball is an old garden shrub that owes its name to the large, nearly globular heads of white flowers that bloom in May or June. The individual flowers are relatively large and all sterile. The oppositely arranged leaves are three to five lobed. *Viburnum* was the Latin name for the wayfaring tree, *V. lantana; opulus,* from *populus,* "a poplar," is of uncertain application; *sterile* alludes to the absence of fruits. Guelder-rose is another common name for this viburnum, a member of the honeysuckle family, Caprifoliaceae. Cultivated for centuries, it was supposed to have originated in Gelderland, a province of the Netherlands, but its natural range embraces not only Europe but Asia and North Africa. There are many British folk names for the snowball: upon occasion it is called cranberry tree, European cranberry bush, and high-bush cranberry (the last better used for the American, *V. trilobum,* which bears red fruits). According to Keeler, the snowball reached America in 1652. References to it, usually as "Guelder Rose," indicate that it was widely known and used in the colonies. (See also high-bush cranberry.)

Snowdrop—*Galanthus nivalis*

The snowdrop is a bulbous plant of the amaryllis family, Amaryllidaceae, with a nodding white flower at the top of each flower stalk, 6-12 inches high. The three larger, outside flower parts are the sepals, the three inner parts, marked with green, the petals. Two or three strap-shaped leaves rise from the base of the plant and die as

the summer advances. Snowdrops may bloom from late January to early March, depending upon the season, often while the snow is on the ground. The generic name is from the Greek *gala,* "milk," and *anthos,* "flower"; *nivalis* is Latin for "snowy." A number of picturesque local names in Britain include fair-maids-of-February, Candlemas bells, and white ladies. The snowdrop, grown by Gerard in his garden and considered native in England, is an introduced species from the continent with a range from the Pyrenees to the Caucasus. "Snow Drops" were grown by Lady Skipwith.

Sour gum—*Nyssa sylvatica*

The sour gum is a deciduous tree native in the eastern United States. In the broadly oval, waxy leaves, 2-5 inches long, more or less rounded at the tip, the branch veins tend to be parallel with the margins, as in the related members of the dogwood family, Cornaceae. The foliage turns a distinctive orange-red in the fall. The bark of

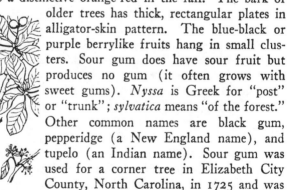

older trees has thick, rectangular plates in alligator-skin pattern. The blue-black or purple berrylike fruits hang in small clusters. Sour gum does have sour fruit but produces no gum (it often grows with sweet gums). *Nyssa* is Greek for "post" or "trunk"; *sylvatica* means "of the forest." Other common names are black gum, pepperidge (a New England name), and tupelo (an Indian name). Sour gum was used for a corner tree in Elizabeth City County, North Carolina, in 1725 and was mentioned by William Byrd in 1733. Peter Kalm commented upon the frequency with which mistletoe was found on this species. Collinson repeatedly asked John Bartram to send specimens and seeds.

Sourwood—*Oxydendrum arboreum*

Sourwood is a low tree with small, white, cup-shaped flowers that grow in terminal clusters in June or July and closely resemble the lily of the valley. The small, dry fruit capsules persist a long time. The oblong leaves, 5-8 inches, taper at both ends, and turn a beautiful scarlet in the fall. They are sour or bitter, and the word "sourwood" was in use by the colonists at least as early as 1709,

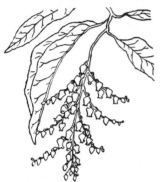

according to the *Dictionary of American English*. The generic name is from the Greek words *oxys*, "acid" or "sour," and *dendron*, "tree"; *arboreum* means "treelike" or "woody." John Bartram listed this native species as "Andromeda arborea — Sorrel-tree," and it was introduced into England under this name in 1752. The natural range is from Pennsylvania southward to Florida, and westward to Indiana and Louisiana. Sourwood belongs to the heath family, Ericaceae.

Spearmint—*Mentha spicata*

Throughout the summer spearmint bears minute, very pale lavender or white flowers in a slender, tapering, pointed spike—often interrupted — at the top of the plant's four-angled stem. The leaves of this common garden mint are mostly stalkless. (Peppermint has short-stalked leaves and a blunt flower spike.) *Mentha* is derived from Minthe, Greek name of a nymph who was turned into an aromatic plant by Persephone in a fit of jealousy; the specific name means "spiked," in reference to the flower cluster. Spearmint is considered native in England though perhaps it was brought from the continent by the Romans. It was planted in Elder William Brewster's garden in Plymouth, Massachusetts, before

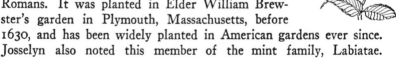

1630, and has been widely planted in American gardens ever since. Josselyn also noted this member of the mint family, Labiatae.

Star-of-Bethlehem—*Ornithogalum umbellatum*

The May-blooming star-of-Bethlehem is a bulbous member of the lily family, Liliaceae. There are three to twelve flowers on short stalks; characteristically the white sepals and petals are striped with

green on the under side. There are six
to nine narrow leaves. To someone,
centuries ago, the whiteness of the star-
shaped flowers must have suggested the
most famous star of Christendom. The
generic name is compounded from the
Greek *ornis,* "bird," and *gala,* "milk,"
but the basis for the coinage is obscure;
umbellatum means "shadow" or "small

umbrella." There are many British folk names for this plant, of
Mediterranean origin and known since the ninth century B.C.
Eleven-o'clock-lady and sleepy Dick are applicable because the flowers
open only when the sun is shining. Peter Collinson sent ornitho-
galums to John Bartram in 1740, and they were advertised in Boston
in 1760. A related species, *O. nutans,* has a thick, erect stalk, with
the lower flowers drooping; *nutans* means "nodding." Both species
grow in Williamsburg gardens, and wild in the vicinity.

Stewartia—*Stewartia malachodendron*

In May, June, or later, this small tree — or better, tall shrub—
bears large, white, cup-shaped camellialike flowers, 3-4 inches across;
the stamens are numerous, and the anthers bluish-purple (if the
anthers are orange, it is the closely related mountain camellia, *S.
pentagyna* or *ovata*). Mark Catesby chose the name, recognized by
Linnaeus, to honor John Stuart, Earl of Bute (1713-1792), a patron
of botanists, among them John Bartram; *malachodendron,* Greek for
"soft tree," was the old generic name for this plant. In 1741, John
Mitchell of Urbanna, Virginia, sent a description of *S. malachodendron* to England. Catesby illustrated it in his *Natural History,*

commenting that he had it from John Clayton in Virginia in 1742. Peter Collinson
wrote John Bartram in 1766 "The Stuartia
flowered for the first time in the Princess
of Wales' Garden, at Kew, which is the
Paradise of our world, where all plants are
found that money or interest can procure."
Stewartia, a member of the tea family,
Theaceae, is a native species, restricted to
southern United States.

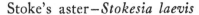

Stoke's aster—*Stokesia laevis*

Jonathan Stokes, a British physician and botanist, is remembered in the common and generic names of this perennial herb; *laevis* means "smooth." The flowers, which bloom in June or July, are almost all colors but yellow and orange; the flower heads, about 1 inch across in the wild members and as much as 4 inches in cultivated forms, have numerous "petals" — really ray florets — that are long, narrow, and more or less curled at the ends; they are distinctly larger at the margin than toward the center. Leaves are long and lance shaped, the basal ones without teeth, the upper ones with a few shallow teeth. The stem is purplish with white, wooly, matted hairs. The plant, a member of the ironweed tribe of the family Compositae, is native to the southern United States. It was introduced into cultivation in England from Carolina in 1766.

Summer phlox—*Phlox paniculata*

This erect garden herb, 3-4 feet tall, has dense terminal clusters of white, pink, or rose tubular flowers—each with five fused petals abruptly formed into a disc at the end of the slender tube. A series of narrow, pointed, short-stalked leaves grow in pairs along the stem. Summer phlox blooms from late June sometimes into September. *Phlox,* Greek word for "flame," was originally applied to a red-flowered species of *Lychnis; paniculata* or "panicles" describes the dense flower clusters. Pink specimens of this native of the southern United States were sent to England in 1732. Collinson wrote: "1744, a new lychnidea, sent by J. Bartram with a large spike of pale reddish purple flowers with peach-shaped leaves, flowered in July and August." The original wild species has been greatly developed by selection and even hybridization with other species of phlox. From the frequency of references by Miller, Hill, and others, we know that this member of the phlox family, Polemoniaceae, became very popular in eighteenth-century English gardens.

Swamp holly—*Ilex decidua*

Before the berries appear, swamp holly is an inconspicuous non-evergreen shrub—not at all like its relative, the American holly tree, *I. opaca.* The dark green leaves are oblong, 1-3 inches long, broadest near the tip, pale and hairy beneath and with sunken veins above. The small, whitish flowers are succeeded by orange-red fruits, mostly on short spurs. The generic name was the Latin name for the holm oak, *Quercus ilex; decidua* means "falling off," and refers to the non-evergreen character of this holly. Deciduous winterberry and possum haw are other common names. As "Prinos deciduus," this holly was introduced into England from Virginia in 1736. A native species in the United States, swamp holly ranges from Virginia to Florida and westward to Texas. It belongs to the holly family, Aquifoliaceae. (See also inkberry, myrtle-leaved holly, winterberry, and yaupon.)

Swamp rose—*Rosa palustris*

The swamp rose, which grows wild throughout the eastern United States, is not restricted to swamps. This species is the *R. carolina* of some authors other than Linnaeus, and thus is often confused with the meadow rose, named *R. carolina* by Linnaeus. The plant is a shrub with seven, rarely nine, finely toothed leaflets, narrowly oblong, 1½-2 inches long. The single pink flowers bloom in June and later, singly or in few-flowered clusters. *Rosa* is the Latin name for rose; *palustris* means "pertaining to a swamp."
In 1738, Peter Collinson asked John Bartram to "send a specimen or two of the Upland Rose and of the Marsh Rose," and in 1751 he listed these varieties in the *Gentleman's Magazine.* The reference may have been to *R. palustris.* It is assumed that this attractive native member of the rose family, Rosaceae, early found a place in colonial gardens.

Sweet bay—*Magnolia virginiana*

Sweet bay, a native shrub with a range from Massachusetts to Texas, is partly evergreen — the degree is influenced by the latitude and conditions in the winter. The leaves, usually narrow-oblong, have a conspicuous whitish film on the lower surface. The white, globose flowers, 2-3 inches across, that come in May, are very fragrant. This member of the magnolia family, Magnoliaceae, is also known as swamp magnolia, swamp laurel, white bay, and beaver tree (beavers were so fond of the root and bark that the colonists used them to bait traps). Bay, from the French *baie,* the Latin *baca,* suggests resemblances to the true bay, or laurel, *Laurus nobilis.* The genus honors Pierre Magnol (1638-1715), director of the botanical garden at Montpelier, France. The specific name indicates the region in which the plant was first collected. As "Magnolia glauca" the sweet bay was sent to England by John Banister in 1688; thereafter it was in constant demand by English horticulturalists. Peter Kalm commented that the scent of the flowers could be detected three quarters of a mile away if the wind were favorable. In *Notes on the State of Virginia,* Jefferson classed the wild sweet bay as an ornamental.

Sweet gum—*Liquidambar styraciflua*

Sweet gum or red gum is an American deciduous tree that ranges along the coast from Connecticut to Florida, to Texas, Mexico, Guatemala, and Venezuela. The star-shaped, rather maplelike, leaves, with five to seven pointed lobes and uniformly saw-toothed margins, are distinctive. Usually the branches have corky warts or ridges; the fruits are stalked, hanging spheres, about an inch in diameter and coarsely spiny. The generic name is from the Latin *liquidus,* "liquid," and the Arabic *ambar,* "fragrant material"; the specific name comes from *styrax,* Greek

for a storax tree, and hence for its resin, and the Latin *fluere,* "to flow." The resinous, fragrant sap, which flows in quantity from the trees south of North Carolina, is used in censers in Central America. Catesby's *Natural History* includes the "Liquid Ambar" which at first he called "Styrax aceris folio." Peter Kalm remarked on the use of sweet gum for furniture and cartwheels, and Jefferson listed it as "useful for fabrication." When William Byrd was running the Dividing Line between Virginia and North Carolina he dispensed "Sweet Gumm," a member of the witch-hazel family, Hamamelidaceae, as a specific for dysentery.

Sweet pepperbush—*Clethra alnifolia*

Sweet pepperbush is a shrub with slender twigs and oblong leaves, 2-4 inches, usually widest near the tip. Starting in July the small, white, fragrant flowers bloom in erect, spikelike clusters. The genus is from *klethra,* the Greek name for the alder, transferred because of the resemblance of the leaves; *alnifolia* is Latin for "alder leaved." Common names include summer sweet, white alder, and spiked alder. A species native from Maine to Florida, sweet pepperbush first reached England in 1731. Bartram included "Clethra or Sweet Spiraea," among the seeds he sent his English patrons. Peter Collinson wrote him, "to my great loss, some prying, knowing people, looked into the cases, and . . . took . . . the Spiraea Alni folio." Jefferson listed "Clethra" as one of the "shrubs not exceeding 10 feet in height." It belongs to the heath family, Ericaceae, together with sourwood and mountain laurel.

Sweet William—*Dianthus barbatus*

Sweet William, probably named in honor of William the Conqueror, is one of the oldest garden plants. A perennial herb, blooming in June, it has dense, round-topped clusters of white, pink, red, or purple flowers, not always fragrant. Each flower is frequently marked with a darker color; the petals are fringed and toothed and usually bearded on the lower surface. The leaves, relatively large and broad for a member of the pink family, Caryophyllaceae, are

opposite on the angled, jointed stems. *Dianthus,* literally "Jove's flower," was applied by Theophrastus to a wild pink; *barbatus,* Latin for "barbed" or "bearded," has reference to the hairs on the petals. Other common names are bunch pink and London pride. Sweet William was introduced into England from "Germany" in 1573; the original home was China and Russia. A familiar plant in colonial gardens, sweet William was advertised for sale in Boston in 1760, grown by Jefferson and Lady Skipwith, and sold by Minton Collins of Richmond in 1793. William Hamilton of Philadelphia had double ones in 1785. (See also carnation and grass pink.)

Sycamore—*Platanus occidentalis*

Peter Kalm noted that the "Virginia maple" was "planted about the houses and in gardens to afford a pleasant shade." Jefferson wrote to Martha Randolph from Philadelphia in July, 1793: "I never before knew the full value of trees. My house is enbosomed in high plane trees, with good grass below, and under them I breakfast, dine, write, read, and receive my company." The American sycamore or plane tree, also known as buttonwood and buttonball, is a big tree with large, coarsely toothed leaves; the base of each leafstalk, hollow and swollen, conceals the new bud. The zig-zag twigs, the piebald bark of older trees, and the fruit — a stalked, hanging sphere, hairy but not spiny—are all distinctive. The name comes from the Greek *sykomorus* for the fig, *Ficus sycomorus; platanus* was the Greek name for the European plane, the ultimate source apparently *platys,* "flat," in reference to the plates of the bark. (The English "sycamore" is a maple, *Acer pseudoplatanus.*) The specific name, which means "western," is in contrast to the Oriental plane, *P. orientalis;* both are members of the small sycamore family, Platanaceae. This rapidly growing tree, especially abundant along streams — which carry the fruits — was well known throughout the colonies.

Tartarian honeysuckle—*Lonicera tatarica*

This tall shrub of the honeysuckle family, Caprifoliaceae, has opposite, ovate to heart-shaped, almost stalkless leaves. In April and May it bears pinkish or white flowers, partly tubular, usually in pairs at the leaf bases; these are followed by shining, thin-skinned red berries. Honeysuckle is said to come from the Anglo-Saxon name *hunisuce,* "privet," also opposite leaved. The genus was named for Adam Lonicer (Lonitzer), a German physician and herbalist (*c.* 1526-86); the specific name refers to Tartary, the plant's original home. Tartarian honeysuckle was introduced into cultivation in England from Russia in 1752 and probably was imported into the colonies before 1770. It has escaped from cultivation and occurs wild from Maine to Kentucky. It should not be confused with the woodbine of British poets, *L. periclymenum,* or with the common honeysuckle of the south, *L. japonica,* introduced from Japan and China about 1806, and now a rampant weed in clearings and along roadsides from Connecticut to Florida. (See also trumpet honeysuckle.)

Tawny daylily—*Hemerocallis fulva*

The tawny daylily is a perennial herb with brown-orange or copper-colored flowers, unspotted. These are funnel shaped, 4 inches across, and grow in small clusters at the top of the stiff flower stalks. The strap-shaped leaves, bending over when mature, and broader than those of the lemon daylily, form rich green clumps. Individual flowers, as with the lemon daylily, *H. flava,* also described in this book, shrivel after a day, hence the common name and *Hemerocallis,* meaning "beautiful for a day"; *fulva* is "orange." The tawny daylily came to England from the "Levant" in 1596; in America it was "used before 1700," according to *Gardens of Colony and State.*

This member of the lily family, Liliaceae, long escaped from cultivation, now grows wild from New Brunswick to Virginia.

Tree box—*Buxus sempervirens arborescens*

Tree box forms a high shrub and grows much faster than the smaller edging box, described on page 32; the leaves, oval, dark green above and paler beneath, are also larger — about 1 inch long. Both the common and generic names are from the Latin, *buxus,* and the Greek, *puxos,* names for this very plant; *sempervirens* means "always green"; *arborescens,* "growing to be a tree." Box has been used ornamentally from the earliest times. Pliny the Younger described the curiously shaped box on his estates in Italy. In Shakespeare's day, box was used in England to dry linen on; musical instruments were made from the hard wood but the principal use of this highly prized shrub has always been ornamental. Captain Ridgeley, of Hampton, Maryland, left a will in 1787 directing that his box gardens be maintained. Box, an introduced species from southern Europe, North Africa, and the Orient, belongs to its own small family, Buxaceae.

Tree peony—*Paeonia suffruticosa*

The tree peony, in contrast to the common herbaceous peony, is a woody shrub. The stem, which bears large, many-petaled flowers in shades of red, sometimes white, branches near the ground. The leaves, much divided, are pale on the undersides. Tree peonies bloom in late March, April, or May, depending upon the weather. On old plants the blooms are numerous. The genus, which includes the herbaceous peony, *P. officinalis,* derives its name ultimately from Paeon, Greek physician-god of healing, in reference to supposed medicinal qualities. The specific name is Latin for "somewhat shrubby." In 1789, white and purple forms were introduced into England as "P. moutan," from China, where they had been esteemed for many centuries. The tree peony belongs to the buttercup family, Ranunculaceae. (See also peony.)

Trumpet creeper—*Campsis radicans*

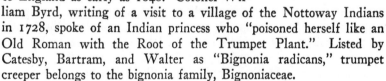

The common name well describes this native vine which creeps over the ground (or on a higher support if it is available) and in July bears clusters of vivid orange-scarlet, trumpet-shaped flowers about 3 inches long. It also is called trumpet vine, trumpet flower, and cow-itch (the basis for this last quite unknown). The generic name is from the Greek *kampsis*, "curvature," in reference to the four curved stamens; *radicans* is Latin for "rooting"— the plant climbs by aerial rootlets. Trumpet creeper has opposite, compound leaves which are divided into seven to eleven ovate leaflets. The fruit, a dry pod, is 5-6 inches long. As *Tecoma radicans,* trumpet creeper was sent to England as early as 1640. Colonel William Byrd, writing of a visit to a village of the Nottoway Indians in 1728, spoke of an Indian princess who "poisoned herself like an Old Roman with the Root of the Trumpet Plant." Listed by Catesby, Bartram, and Walter as "Bignonia radicans," trumpet creeper belongs to the bignonia family, Bignoniaceae.

Trumpet honeysuckle—*Lonicera sempervirens*

Trumpet honeysuckle, or coral honeysuckle as it is often called, is a native vine with broadly ovate, stalkless leaves, 2-3 inches long—

the upper leaves broadly joined at their bases to form discs. The narrowly tubular flowers that bloom, from April through the summer, in clusters at the ends of the branches, are 2 inches long, scarlet or orange-red without, yellow within. The fruit is an orange or scarlet berry. Trumpet alludes to the shape of the flowers; honeysuckle is from the Anglo-Saxon name for privet, *hunisuce.* The genus was named for a sixteenth-century German physician and herbalist; *sempervirens* means "evergreen." There are many references to this member of the honeysuckle family, Caprifoliaceae: William Byrd wrote of trumpet honeysuckle in 1728; Jefferson listed it as an ornamental in 1781. John Bartram and Prince listed it; Lady Skipwith had both "English, and Red Trumpet Honeysuckle" at Prestwould. (See also Tartarian honeysuckle.)

Tulip — *Tulipa* spp.

Familiar in the spring is the large solitary flower of the tulip, with six perianth parts (three petals and three sepals similarly colored) on a thick green flower stalk, with basal, clasping leaves. Tulips were cultivated in Asia Minor for centuries before the colonial period in America. The Turks were the first to breed this bulbous member of the lily family, Liliaceae. Credit is given to Busbequius, Austrian ambassador to Constantinople, for bringing the tulip to Vienna in 1554. The Dutch soon became tulip specialists; tulipomania swept Holland, reaching its peak in the four years following 1634, when some bulbs fetched fantastic prices. John Custis of Williamsburg imported bulbs from Europe in 1725 and 1726. John Bartram received "tulip roots" from Collinson in 1738 and hoped that "there may be some differing from what we have already." By 1760, fifty varieties were advertised for sale in Boston. Tulip comes from a Persian word *thoulyban,* "turban," in reference to the shape of the inverted flower. Most garden tulips are derived from crosses of *T. suaveolens* and *T. gesneriana* and are indeterminable to species.

Tulip tree — *Liriodendron tulipifera*

The tall-growing tulip tree has greenish-yellow flowers somewhat like tulips in shape and size. The large leaves, broadly notched inwardly at the tip, are very distinctive. The generic name is from the Greek *leirion,* "lily," and *dendron,* "tree"; the specific name is Latin for "tulip-bearing." Other common names are tulip poplar, yellow poplar, and whitewood. Records of this native tree are early and numerous: in his *Natural History of Virginia,* William Byrd

wrote "Everyone has some of these trees in his gardens and around the house, for ornament and pleasure." Indians and early settlers in Virginia made dugouts of this tree, as noted by Peter Kalm, who also said the Delaware Swedes called it "Canoe tree." The bark of the roots was used in the treatment of fevers, especially malaria. The tulip tree belongs to the magnolia family, Magnoliaceae.

Turtlehead—*Chelone glabra*

The turtlehead, also sometimes called snakehead, codhead, shell-flower, and balmony, is a native member of the snapdragon family, Scrophulariaceae, that was early brought into colonial gardens. The white, sometimes pink, broadly tubular and two-lipped flowers grow in a short, showy, terminal cluster flowering all summer. Each is like a gaping turtle's beak and head, hence the generic name *Chelone,* from the Greek word for tortoise or turtle; the Latin *glabra,* "smooth," refers to the opposite, saw-toothed leaves, which are nearly stalkless. The plant, 1-2 feet tall, was used by the American Indians as a vermifuge and in other medicinal ways. John Clayton cultivated it in his garden in what is now Mathews County, Virginia. In 1764 he wrote Bartram "I have not, at this time any of the seed . . . of the red Chelone," but the following year he wrote again "I now send you the seed of the red-flowered Chelone." This species was listed in Clayton's *Flora Virginica* and included in Walter's *Flora Caroliniana.*

Valerian—*Valeriana officinalis*

Valerian, a type member of its own family, Valerianaceae, is a tall perennial, an old-time garden plant, with broadly lance-shaped leaves, the upper ones considerably cut or lobed. The small tubular flowers, appearing in May and June, are usually pink-red, but sometimes lavender or whitish. The flowers, which grow in roundish clusters

at the top of the plant and at the ends of branch stems, have a pronounced spicy fragrance and *three* stamens. (If only *one* stamen is present in individual flowers, it is the red valerian, *Centranthus ruber.*) Both the common and generic names are from the Latin *valere,* "to be strong," in reference to medicinal properties; the specific name has similar connotations. The root stocks still provide an ingredient for tonics and nerve remedies. Other common names include common valerian, cat's valerian, and St.-George's-herb. Valerian, a native of Europe and adjacent Asia, was grown by John Gerard in his London garden. Thomas Jefferson listed a valerian as a "medicinal plant" in his *Notes on the State of Virginia.*

Veronica—*Veronica maritima*

This veronica, also known as *V. longifolia,* reached England from Sweden in 1570, and was probably introduced on this side of the Atlantic early in the colonial period. The common and generic names for this old garden plant, also known as clump speedwell, perhaps are after St. Veronica, although older writers are uncertain; *maritima,* "pertaining to the sea," associates the plant with salt marshes. Veronica is a perennial herb with small, tubular flowers, deep blue, that bloom from May through the summer in a dense terminal cluster. Each small flower has two sta-  mens. The leaves are oblong, tapering, 3-4 inches long, and sharply toothed. The whole plant, densely growing, attains a height of 2-3 feet. This member of the snapdragon family, Scrophulariaceae, originally from Europe and northern Asia, is now naturalized in America.

Violet—*Viola sororia*

This perennial violet, one of many species of the genus *Viola,* in the violet family, Violaceae, is equally at home in moist meadows, woodlands, and gardens from Quebec to the Carolinas. One of the most familiar of the native violets in the vicinity of

Williamsburg, undoubtedly it was appreciated in colonial days. The flowers are purple-violet to lavender, occasionally white. The basal leaves, triangular to broadly heart shaped and not lobed, are borne on an underground stem; the leafstalks, 1-4 inches, characteristically are downy. *Viola* was the Latin name for the violet, said to be from the Greek

maiden, Ion or Io, for whom violets were created as herbage when Zeus changed her into a heifer to conceal her from his jealous wife; *sororia* is from *soror,* "sister," perhaps in reference to the clusters of flowers on their separate stalks. Jefferson mentioned violets several times in his *Garden Book,* 1767.

Virginia scrub pine—*Pinus virginiana*

The Virginia scrub pine, sometimes called the Jersey scrub pine, is an evergreen tree with relatively short, thickish needles, 1½-3 inches, two to a bundle. (The other local pine in Tidewater Virginia is the loblolly pine, which has three, longer needles to a bundle. The white pine, which has been brought from the Blue Ridge, has *five* bluish-green needles per bundle.) *Pinus* is the old Latin name for pine; the specific name pertains to the region typical for this tree. Peter Kalm referred to a pine with "double leaves and oblong cone. . . . The English to distinguish it, call it the Jersey pine."

Schoepf wrote of "the Rosemary-Pine, so called, which has but two needles, and short ones," and added "It is difficult to get a clear notion of the many names, varieties and sub-varieties of this region [North Carolina]."Thomas Jefferson listed "Yellow pine. Pinus Virginica" as "useful for fabrication." One must perhaps be an expert to identify all pines, but in the vicinity of Williamsburg, only the three species described in this book are characteristic. The Virginia scrub pine, one of the many members of the pine family, Pinaceae, ranges from southern New York to Indiana and south to Georgia and Alabama.

Washington thorn—*Crataegus phaenopyrum*

At Mount Vernon George Washington made considerable use of this small dense tree, which has slender spines growing from the bases of broadly ovate or triangular leaves, three to five lobed and sharp toothed.

May-blooming white flowers, like tiny roses, come in dense clusters, followed by bright red fruits resembling minute apples. *Crataegus* is from the Greek *krataigos,* for a flowering thorn of this group—the ultimate derivation being from *kratos,* or "strength," in reference to the hardness of the wood; the specific name apparently is from two Greek words that mean "showy wheat," suggested by the large clusters of bright red fruits. John Bartram sent Peter Collinson both a black-berried and a red-berried crataegus in 1738. Extensive fences of the Washington thorn were planted at Monticello in 1805. This hawthorn, which belongs to the rose family, Rosaceae, is a native species that extends from Virginia to Alabama and Missouri.

Wax myrtle—*Myrica cerifera*

The native shrub, wax myrtle, is so named because its fruits, favorite food of the myrtle warbler, yield an abundance of wax from which candles can still be made; it resembles the true myrtle in being evergreen. Other common names include bay-berry, candleberry, and tallow shrub. Linnaeus took the generic name from the Greek *myrike,* an old Hellenic name for some aromatic shrub, probably the tamarisk; *cerifera* is Latin for "wax-bearing." The leaves are somewhat leathery, elongate-

oblong, usually 2-4 inches long, often with a few sawlike teeth at the tip; the surfaces, dark green above and lighter beneath, have yellow resin dots. The fruit, a waxy, greenish-gray, stalkless berry, grows in dense clusters close to the stem. Wax myrtle was introduced into

England in 1699 and was described at length in Robert Beverley's *History of Virginia*. John Bartram sent seeds each year over a long period to his English patrons. There are numerous references by the early botanists to this member of the sweet-gale family, Myricaceae, which ranges along the coastal plain from New Jersey to Florida and Texas.

Weeping willow—*Salix babylonica*

The easily rooted weeping willow, which belongs to the willow family, Salicaceae, is a Chinese species that reached England by way of the Levant in 1730. The adjective "weeping" is often applied to plants with pendulous or drooping branches. *Salix* is the Latin name for willow; *babylonica* is after the willows of Babylon (Psalm 137), which, however, were really *Populus euphratica*. Another common name is Napoleon's willow, because many of these trees in the United States are said to have come from St. Helena. The weeping willow has long, slender, drooping twigs, with long, narrow leaves that taper at each end. Washington,  in his diary of 1785, mentions the weeping willow, and, according to Jefferson, the original graveyard at Monticello (1773) was surrounded by weeping willows. There are numerous references in Jefferson's writings to this species, which was also listd in Prince's catalogue of 1790.

Western catalpa—*Catalpa speciosa*

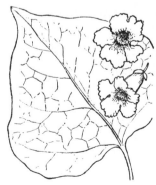 This large native tree, with a natural range from Arkansas to Illinois and south to Louisiana and Mississippi, has very large, broadly heart-shaped or triangular leaves which taper to a point at the end. These grow in threes, as well as in opposite pairs, on stout twigs. Large, white, trumpet-shaped flowers come in June, singly or in small clusters, and are more or less marked with lines of purple-brown. The fruit is a long,

thin, cylindrical pod, about a foot in length, which contains many papery, winged seeds. The bark is thick and ridged, distinguishing this species from the common catalpa (described on page 27), which has thin, scaly bark on mature trees, and also bears flowers in larger clusters. According to one authority the western catalpa was introduced along the Atlantic Coast in the colonial period and was probably better known than the common catalpa, although at present the earliest record of cultivation is 1754. Catalpa comes from the Indian name; *speciosa* means "showy," in reference to the flowers. Catalpas belong to the largely tropical family Bignoniaceae.

White-flowered jasmine — *Jasminum officinale*

This low shrub with long, running branches bears fragrant white flowers in May. These are tubular, flat lobed at the end, about an inch across, and bloom in convex terminal clusters of two to ten flowers. The leaves are divided into five to seven shiny leaflets. Introduced into cultivation in England from the East Indies in 1548, it is a much  older plant than the common yellow jasmine. The generic name is the Latinized form of *ysmyn,* the ancient Persian or Arabic word for these plants; the specific name has connotations of medicinal or other useful qualities — in this instance, a source of perfume. Washington in his diary called it "Persian Jessamine," Lady Skipwith had "white jasmine," and Thomas Jefferson referred to both "jasmine white" and "yellow." (The latter, however, was not the *J. nudiflorum* of present-day gardens but the Carolina jessamine, *Gelsemium sempervirens.*) An introduced species from Asia, the white-flowered jasmine is a member of the olive family, Oleaceae.

White oak — *Quercus alba*

Mature trees of the white oak have bark decidedly lighter in color than that of the black-oak group (including the scarlet oak described on page 73). Linnaeus gave the genus the Latin common name for an oak; *alba* means "white." The white oak, one of the best-known native members of the beech or oak family, Fagaceae, has smooth leaves with five to nine *rounded* lobes and *no* bristles. When mature,

94

it is a tall, broad-crowned tree. Typically, on younger trees especially, many dead leaves remain attached throughout the winter. From the Indians the early colonists learned to boil and eat the large acorns. Sometimes oil was skimmed off and used as liniment "to supple their joynts." The white oak, closest to the English oak, was mentioned by almost all the early plantsmen. It provided a

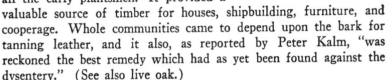

valuable source of timber for houses, shipbuilding, furniture, and cooperage. Whole communities came to depend upon the bark for tanning leather, and it also, as reported by Peter Kalm, "was reckoned the best remedy which had as yet been found against the dysentery." (See also live oak.)

White pine—*Pinus strobus*

The white pine, an evergreen tree belonging to the pine family, Pinaceae, has slender, blue-green needles in bundles of five. *Pinus* was the Latin name for the pine; *strobus* was a pre-Linnaean genus. This species, which ranges from Newfoundland south in the mountains to Georgia, is also known as northern white pine, eastern white pine, and Weymouth pine — the last because it was sent to England

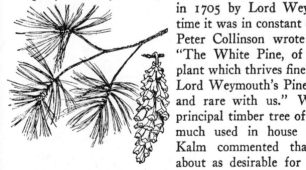

in 1705 by Lord Weymouth. From that time it was in constant demand in England. Peter Collinson wrote to John Bartram: "The White Pine, of which thee sent a plant which thrives finely, is called here ... Lord Weymouth's Pine. This sort is scarce and rare with us." White pine was the principal timber tree of New England, and much used in house construction; Peter Kalm commented that white pine was about as desirable for shingles as cypress.

The inner bark and cambium was used as a masticatory by the Indians, and also dried to make breadstuffs; the young shoots were peeled and candied by the settlers of New England, where it was the model for the "Pine Tree Shillings" of Massachusetts. (See also loblolly pine and Virginia scrub pine.)

Willow oak—*Quercus phellos*

The native willow oak ranges along the coast from Long Island to Florida and westward to Texas. The lustrous, pale green leaves, narrow and willowlike, 3-5 inches long and 1 inch wide — each leaf with a bristle at the tip — exemplify those of the narrow-leaved, non-evergreen oak group. (In contrast, see both the white oak and the live oak, described in this book.) *Phellos,* the Greek word for cork, was a pre-Linnaean generic name for the related cork oak, *Q. suber.* Another common name, peach oak, refers also to the leaves; pig oak is an allusion to the use of acorns of various oaks as "mast" fed to pigs. Schoepf wrote that "the swamp oak with the willow leaf . . . grows to be a strong and comely tree." The willow oak, member of the beech family, Fagaceae, was esteemed by Jefferson. Large specimen trees grow on many James River estates, and it is, today, a prominent street tree in Richmond. This species was cultivated in England after 1723.

Winterberry—*Ilex verticillata*

Winterberry is a deciduous shrub of the holly family, Aquifoliaceae, with narrowly oval leaves, 1½-3 inches long, very finely toothed, and usually hairy underneath. The bright red berries, clustered along the stem, are persistent and conspicuous in winter—hence the common name. *Ilex* was the Latin name for the holm oak, *Quercus ilex; verticillata* means "verticillate," or "whorled," in this case referring to the clustered berries. Other common names include black alder, dogberry, feverbush, whorled winterberry, and Michigan holly. This shrub first reached England in 1736; it was among the one hundred and fifty kinds of seeds which John

Bartram was requested to gather and send to Peter Collinson and other patrons in England. In 1758, Dr. Garden also sent "Aquifolium fruct. verticillat. . . . a much prettier tree than Mr. Catesby's Dahoon holly." Winterberry is native in the eastern United States.

Yarrow—*Achillea millefolium*

Yarrow is a perennial herb, a weed rarely cultivated now except in a variety such as the pink-flowered *A. millefolium roseum*. However, William Wood, who traveled in New England 1629-33, commented on "perennial yarrow" in planted gardens. Peter Kalm noted it both in Philadelphia and Montreal. Yarrow has finely divided or cut leaves. The pink or white flower heads bloom in May and June, often throughout the summer, with minute florets in a spreading, flat-topped cluster. The old English name "yarrow" is from the Anglo-Saxon *gearuwe*. The genus was named by Linneaus for Achilles, who supposedly healed his wounds with this plant; the specific name means "thousand leaved," in reference to the much cut foliage. Among the many other common names are milfoil, nosebleed, and sneezewort. Yarrow, native in Europe and Asia, is now extensively naturalized in North America. It is a member of the camomile tribe of the composite family, Compositae.

Yaupon—*Ilex vomitoria*

"It makes a very good and most beautiful hedge and may be kept as short and neat as the Box" wrote Dr. Garden of yaupon. In another letter, to John Ellis, he said "What is here called the *Cassine* is a species of the Ilex. . . . Indians make what they call their Black Drink of it." Yaupon, variously spelled yapon, youpon, yupon, and japon, is a native evergreen member of the holly family, Aquifoliaceae. The leaves are elongate-oblong, blunt at the tip, 1-1½ inches long, with wavy-toothed margins. Flowers in May are succeeded by small, green berries, turning scarlet in the fall, which grow in dense clusters on the old wood. *Vomitoria* refers to the emetic qualities of the strong brew made by the Indians from this species, allied to maté, *I. paraguayensis*. Colonists made tea from yaupon, which contains caffeine, sometimes mixing it with persimmon beer and herbs. Peter Collinson asked John Custis of Williamsburg to send him "cherries of Caessenna or yapon," reporting at the same time Bartram's high opinion of Custis' garden. Yaupon grows along the coast from Virginia to Florida, westward to Texas and Arkansas.

Yellow iris—*Iris pseudacorus*

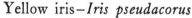

The generic and common names are from the classical rainbow goddess Iris; the specific name, which means "false acorus," refers to sweet flag. Known also as flower-de-luce, the yellow iris of Europe, Asia, and North Africa has several dozen local folk names in England alone. It is a perennial member of the iris family, Iridaceae; the yellow flowers come in May, with the three outer perianth segments drooping, the three inner ones erect, all with a claw. According to legend, the pious young crusader Louis VII adopted this iris as the flower of his house, and it eventually became the fleur-de-lis of France. As "Flower de luce," Jefferson recorded it "just opening" on May 28, 1767, and his Account Book shows that he planned to have it at Monticello. There are innumerable references to the flower in the writings of Chaucer, Spenser, Ben Jonson, Francis Bacon, Shakespeare, and others. (See also blue iris.)

Yellow wood—*Cladrastis lutea*

Yellow wood is rare even on the limestone slopes of the mountains of Tennessee, Kentucky, and North Carolina, where it is native. The compound leaves of this member of the Leguminosae, or bean family, have seven to nine large leaflets, each 3-4 inches long. The white flowers which appear in late spring after the leaves, are sweet-pealike and grow in drooping clusters, resembling those of the locust. Yellow wood owes its name to the clear yellow dye that can be obtained from the wood, itself yellow in color. The generic name is compounded from the Greek words

98

klados, "branch," and *thraustos,* "fragile," in reference to the brittleness of the twigs; *lutea* means "yellow." Other names include Kentucky yellow wood, virgilia, and gopherwood. Washington mentioned yellow wood in his diary. A tree belonging to this species which John Bartram planted in his Philadelphia garden was still alive in 1925.

Yucca—*Yucca filamentosa*

The native yucca is a perennial plant with a large clump of stiff, irislike leaves. The deep cup-shaped white flowers which bloom in June form a large cluster at the top of a stalk as tall as 12 feet. The common and generic names are the Latinized version of the Spanish vernacular name for some other plant; *filamentosa,* from *filum,* "thread," refers to the characteristic threads of the leaf margins. Spanish bayonet and Adam's-needle are other common names. Yucca is included in Jefferson's garden list of 1794 as beargrass. Dr. Garden, who sent seeds to John Whitworth in 1757, described it as "very beautiful." Schoepf said that "The Yucca filamentosa L. was now often to be seen in the woods [of North Carolina]. Its leaves can be cut into threads, thin and strong, of which the people make use for various household purposes." With a natural range from North Carolina to Florida and Mississippi, this yucca, a member of the lily family, Liliaceae, is now the commonest species of the genus along the Atlantic coast into New England.

INDEX

Wild honeysuckle. *See* pinkster, 67
Wild hops. *See* clematis, 25
Wild hydrangea. *See* hydrangea, 51
Wild sweet William. *See* blue phlox, 17
Wild woodbine. *See* Carolina jessamine, 21
Willow, weeping, 93
Willow oak, 96
Winterberry, 96. *See also* inkberry, 51
Winterberry, deciduous. *See* swamp holly, 81
Winter daffodil. *See* fall daffodil, 36

Wisteria, American, 13
Wisteria frutescens, 13

Yarrow, 97
Yaupon, 97
Yellow daisy. *See* black-eyed Susan, 16
Yellow iris, 98
Yellow locust. *See* locust, 57
Yellow poplar. *See* tulip tree, 88
Yellow wood, 98
Yew, English, 35
Yucca, 99
Yucca filamentosa, 99

A CATALOG OF SELECTED DOVER
BOOKS IN ALL FIELDS OF INTEREST

CONCERNING THE SPIRITUAL IN ART, Wassily Kandinsky. Pioneering work by father of abstract art. Thoughts on color theory, nature of art. Analysis of earlier masters. 12 illustrations. 80pp. of text. 5⅜ × 8½.   23411-8 Pa. $3.95

ANIMALS: 1,419 Copyright-Free Illustrations of Mammals, Birds, Fish, Insects, etc., Jim Harter (ed.). Clear wood engravings present, in extremely lifelike poses, over 1,000 species of animals. One of the most extensive pictorial sourcebooks of its kind. Captions. Index. 284pp. 9 × 12.   23766-4 Pa. $12.95

CELTIC ART: The Methods of Construction, George Bain. Simple geometric techniques for making Celtic interlacements, spirals, Kells-type initials, animals, humans, etc. Over 500 illustrations. 160pp. 9 × 12. (USO)   22923-8 Pa. $9.95

AN ATLAS OF ANATOMY FOR ARTISTS, Fritz Schider. Most thorough reference work on art anatomy in the world. Hundreds of illustrations, including selections from works by Vesalius, Leonardo, Goya, Ingres, Michelangelo, others. 593 illustrations. 192pp. 7⅛ × 10¼.   20241-0 Pa. $9.95

CELTIC HAND STROKE-BY-STROKE (Irish Half-Uncial from "The Book of Kells"): An Arthur Baker Calligraphy Manual, Arthur Baker. Complete guide to creating each letter of the alphabet in distinctive Celtic manner. Covers hand position, strokes, pens, inks, paper, more. Illustrated. 48pp. 8¼ × 11.

24336-2 Pa. $3.95

EASY ORIGAMI, John Montroll. Charming collection of 32 projects (hat, cup, pelican, piano, swan, many more) specially designed for the novice origami hobbyist. Clearly illustrated easy-to-follow instructions insure that even beginning papercrafters will achieve successful results. 48pp. 8¼ × 11.   27298-2 Pa. $2.95

THE COMPLETE BOOK OF BIRDHOUSE CONSTRUCTION FOR WOOD-WORKERS, Scott D. Campbell. Detailed instructions, illustrations, tables. Also data on bird habitat and instinct patterns. Bibliography. 3 tables. 63 illustrations in 15 figures. 48pp. 5¼ × 8½.   24407-5 Pa. $1.95

BLOOMINGDALE'S ILLUSTRATED 1886 CATALOG: Fashions, Dry Goods and Housewares, Bloomingdale Brothers. Famed merchants' extremely rare catalog depicting about 1,700 products: clothing, housewares, firearms, dry goods, jewelry, more. Invaluable for dating, identifying vintage items. Also, copyright-free graphics for artists, designers. Co-published with Henry Ford Museum & Greenfield Village. 160pp. 8¼ × 11.   25780-0 Pa. $9.95

HISTORIC COSTUME IN PICTURES, Braun & Schneider. Over 1,450 costumed figures in clearly detailed engravings—from dawn of civilization to end of 19th century. Captions. Many folk costumes. 256pp. 8⅜ × 11¾.   23150-X Pa. $11.95

STICKLEY CRAFTSMAN FURNITURE CATALOGS, Gustav Stickley and L. & J. G. Stickley. Beautiful, functional furniture in two authentic catalogs from 1910. 594 illustrations, including 277 photos, show settles, rockers, armchairs, reclining chairs, bookcases, desks, tables. 183pp. 6½ × 9¼. 23838-5 Pa. $9.95

AMERICAN LOCOMOTIVES IN HISTORIC PHOTOGRAPHS: 1858 to 1949, Ron Ziel (ed.). A rare collection of 126 meticulously detailed official photographs, called "builder portraits," of American locomotives that majestically chronicle the rise of steam locomotive power in America. Introduction. Detailed captions. xi + 129pp. 9 × 12. 27393-8 Pa. $12.95

AMERICA'S LIGHTHOUSES: An Illustrated History, Francis Ross Holland, Jr. Delightfully written, profusely illustrated fact-filled survey of over 200 American lighthouses since 1716. History, anecdotes, technological advances, more. 240pp. 8 × 10¾. 25576-X Pa. $11.95

TOWARDS A NEW ARCHITECTURE, Le Corbusier. Pioneering manifesto by founder of "International School." Technical and aesthetic theories, views of industry, economics, relation of form to function, "mass-production split" and much more. Profusely illustrated. 320pp. 6⅛ × 9¼. (USO) 25023-7 Pa. $9.95

HOW THE OTHER HALF LIVES, Jacob Riis. Famous journalistic record, exposing poverty and degradation of New York slums around 1900, by major social reformer. 100 striking and influential photographs. 233pp. 10 × 7⅞. 22012-5 Pa $10.95

FRUIT KEY AND TWIG KEY TO TREES AND SHRUBS, William M. Harlow. One of the handiest and most widely used identification aids. Fruit key covers 120 deciduous and evergreen species; twig key 160 deciduous species. Easily used. Over 300 photographs. 126pp. 5⅜ × 8½. 20511-8 Pa. $3.95

COMMON BIRD SONGS, Dr. Donald J. Borror. Songs of 60 most common U.S. birds: robins, sparrows, cardinals, bluejays, finches, more—arranged in order of increasing complexity. Up to 9 variations of songs of each species.
Cassette and manual 99911-4 $8.95

ORCHIDS AS HOUSE PLANTS, Rebecca Tyson Northen. Grow cattleyas and many other kinds of orchids—in a window, in a case, or under artificial light. 63 illustrations. 148pp. 5⅜ × 8½. 23261-1 Pa. $4.95

MONSTER MAZES, Dave Phillips. Masterful mazes at four levels of difficulty. Avoid deadly perils and evil creatures to find magical treasures. Solutions for all 32 exciting illustrated puzzles. 48pp. 8¼ × 11. 26005-4 Pa. $2.95

MOZART'S DON GIOVANNI (DOVER OPERA LIBRETTO SERIES), Wolfgang Amadeus Mozart. Introduced and translated by Ellen H. Bleiler. Standard Italian libretto, with complete English translation. Convenient and thoroughly portable—an ideal companion for reading along with a recording or the performance itself. Introduction. List of characters. Plot summary. 121pp. 5¼ × 8½.
24944-1 Pa. $2.95

TECHNICAL MANUAL AND DICTIONARY OF CLASSICAL BALLET, Gail Grant. Defines, explains, comments on steps, movements, poses and concepts. 15-page pictorial section. Basic book for student, viewer. 127pp. 5⅜ × 8½.
21843-0 Pa. $4.95

BRASS INSTRUMENTS: Their History and Development, Anthony Baines. Authoritative, updated survey of the evolution of trumpets, trombones, bugles, cornets, French horns, tubas and other brass wind instruments. Over 140 illustrations and 48 music examples. Corrected and updated by author. New preface. Bibliography. 320pp. 5⅜ × 8½. 27574-4 Pa. $9.95

HOLLYWOOD GLAMOR PORTRAITS, John Kobal (ed.). 145 photos from 1926–49. Harlow, Gable, Bogart, Bacall; 94 stars in all. Full background on photographers, technical aspects. 160pp. 8⅜ × 11¼. 23352-9 Pa. $11.95

MAX AND MORITZ, Wilhelm Busch. Great humor classic in both German and English. Also 10 other works: "Cat and Mouse," "Plisch and Plumm," etc. 216pp. 5⅜ × 8½. 20181-3 Pa. $5.95

THE RAVEN AND OTHER FAVORITE POEMS, Edgar Allan Poe. Over 40 of the author's most memorable poems: "The Bells," "Ulalume," "Israfel," "To Helen," "The Conqueror Worm," "Eldorado," "Annabel Lee," many more. Alphabetic lists of titles and first lines. 64pp. 5³⁄₁₆ × 8¼. 26685-0 Pa. $1.00

SEVEN SCIENCE FICTION NOVELS, H. G. Wells. The standard collection of the great novels. Complete, unabridged. First Men in the Moon, Island of Dr. Moreau, War of the Worlds, Food of the Gods, Invisible Man, Time Machine, In the Days of the Comet. Total of 1,015pp. 5⅜ × 8½. (USO) 20264-X Clothbd. $29.95

AMULETS AND SUPERSTITIONS, E. A. Wallis Budge. Comprehensive discourse on origin, powers of amulets in many ancient cultures: Arab, Persian, Babylonian, Assyrian, Egyptian, Gnostic, Hebrew, Phoenician, Syriac, etc. Covers cross, swastika, crucifix, seals, rings, stones, etc. 584pp. 5⅜ × 8½. 23573-4 Pa. $12.95

RUSSIAN STORIES/PYCCKNE PACCKA3bl: A Dual-Language Book, edited by Gleb Struve. Twelve tales by such masters as Chekhov, Tolstoy, Dostoevsky, Pushkin, others. Excellent word-for-word English translations on facing pages, plus teaching and study aids, Russian/English vocabulary, biographical/critical introductions, more. 416pp. 5⅜ × 8½. 26244-8 Pa. $8.95

PHILADELPHIA THEN AND NOW: 60 Sites Photographed in the Past and Present, Kenneth Finkel and Susan Oyama. Rare photographs of City Hall, Logan Square, Independence Hall, Betsy Ross House, other landmarks juxtaposed with contemporary views. Captures changing face of historic city. Introduction. Captions. 128pp. 8¼ × 11. 25790-8 Pa. $9.95

AIA ARCHITECTURAL GUIDE TO NASSAU AND SUFFOLK COUNTIES, LONG ISLAND, The American Institute of Architects, Long Island Chapter, and the Society for the Preservation of Long Island Antiquities. Comprehensive, well-researched and generously illustrated volume brings to life over three centuries of Long Island's great architectural heritage. More than 240 photographs with authoritative, extensively detailed captions. 176pp. 8¼ × 11. 26946-9 Pa. $14.95

NORTH AMERICAN INDIAN LIFE: Customs and Traditions of 23 Tribes, Elsie Clews Parsons (ed.). 27 fictionalized essays by noted anthropologists examine religion, customs, government, additional facets of life among the Winnebago, Crow, Zuni, Eskimo, other tribes. 480pp. 6⅛ × 9¼. 27377-6 Pa. $10.95

FRANK LLOYD WRIGHT'S HOLLYHOCK HOUSE, Donald Hoffmann. Lavishly illustrated, carefully documented study of one of Wright's most controversial residential designs. Over 120 photographs, floor plans, elevations, etc. Detailed perceptive text by noted Wright scholar. Index. 128pp. 9¼ × 10¾.
27133-1 Pa. $11.95

THE MALE AND FEMALE FIGURE IN MOTION: 60 Classic Photographic Sequences, Eadweard Muybridge. 60 true-action photographs of men and women walking, running, climbing, bending, turning, etc., reproduced from rare 19th-century masterpiece. vi + 121pp. 9 × 12.
24745-7 Pa. $10.95

1001 QUESTIONS ANSWERED ABOUT THE SEASHORE, N. J. Berrill and Jacquelyn Berrill. Queries answered about dolphins, sea snails, sponges, starfish, fishes, shore birds, many others. Covers appearance, breeding, growth, feeding, much more. 305pp. 5¼ × 8¼.
23366-9 Pa. $7.95

GUIDE TO OWL WATCHING IN NORTH AMERICA, Donald S. Heintzelman. Superb guide offers complete data and descriptions of 19 species: barn owl, screech owl, snowy owl, many more. Expert coverage of owl-watching equipment, conservation, migrations and invasions, etc. Guide to observing sites. 84 illustrations. xiii + 193pp. 5⅜ × 8½.
27344-X Pa. $8.95

MEDICINAL AND OTHER USES OF NORTH AMERICAN PLANTS: A Historical Survey with Special Reference to the Eastern Indian Tribes, Charlotte Erichsen-Brown. Chronological historical citations document 500 years of usage of plants, trees, shrubs native to eastern Canada, northeastern U.S. Also complete identifying information. 343 illustrations. 544pp. 6½ × 9¼.
25951-X Pa. $12.95

STORYBOOK MAZES, Dave Phillips. 23 stories and mazes on two-page spreads: Wizard of Oz, Treasure Island, Robin Hood, etc. Solutions. 64pp. 8¼ × 11.
23628-5 Pa. $2.95

NEGRO FOLK MUSIC, U.S.A., Harold Courlander. Noted folklorist's scholarly yet readable analysis of rich and varied musical tradition. Includes authentic versions of over 40 folk songs. Valuable bibliography and discography. xi + 324pp. 5⅜ × 8½.
27350-4 Pa. $7.95

MOVIE-STAR PORTRAITS OF THE FORTIES, John Kobal (ed.). 163 glamor, studio photos of 106 stars of the 1940s: Rita Hayworth, Ava Gardner, Marlon Brando, Clark Gable, many more. 176pp. 8⅜ × 11¼.
23546-7 Pa. $11.95

BENCHLEY LOST AND FOUND, Robert Benchley. Finest humor from early 30s, about pet peeves, child psychologists, post office and others. Mostly unavailable elsewhere. 73 illustrations by Peter Arno and others. 183pp. 5⅜ × 8½.
22410-4 Pa. $5.95

YEKL and THE IMPORTED BRIDEGROOM AND OTHER STORIES OF YIDDISH NEW YORK, Abraham Cahan. Film Hester Street based on Yekl (1896). Novel, other stories among first about Jewish immigrants on N.Y.'s East Side. 240pp. 5⅜ × 8½.
22427-9 Pa. $6.95

SELECTED POEMS, Walt Whitman. Generous sampling from *Leaves of Grass.* Twenty-four poems include "I Hear America Singing," "Song of the Open Road," "I Sing the Body Electric," "When Lilacs Last in the Dooryard Bloom'd," "O Captain! My Captain!"—all reprinted from an authoritative edition. Lists of titles and first lines. 128pp. 5³⁄₁₆ × 8¼.
26878-0 Pa. $1.00

THE BEST TALES OF HOFFMANN, E. T. A. Hoffmann. 10 of Hoffmann's most important stories: "Nutcracker and the King of Mice," "The Golden Flowerpot," etc. 458pp. 5⅜ × 8½. 21793-0 Pa. $8.95

FROM FETISH TO GOD IN ANCIENT EGYPT, E. A. Wallis Budge. Rich detailed survey of Egyptian conception of "God" and gods, magic, cult of animals, Osiris, more. Also, superb English translations of hymns and legends. 240 illustrations. 545pp. 5⅜ × 8½. 25803-3 Pa. $11.95

FRENCH STORIES/CONTES FRANÇAIS: A Dual-Language Book, Wallace Fowlie. Ten stories by French masters, Voltaire to Camus: "Micromegas" by Voltaire; "The Atheist's Mass" by Balzac; "Minuet" by de Maupassant; "The Guest" by Camus, six more. Excellent English translations on facing pages. Also French-English vocabulary list, exercises, more. 352pp. 5⅜ × 8½. 26443-2 Pa. $8.95

CHICAGO AT THE TURN OF THE CENTURY IN PHOTOGRAPHS: 122 Historic Views from the Collections of the Chicago Historical Society, Larry A. Viskochil. Rare large-format prints offer detailed views of City Hall, State Street, the Loop, Hull House, Union Station, many other landmarks, circa 1904–1913. Introduction. Captions. Maps. 144pp. 9⅜ × 12¼. 24656-6 Pa. $12.95

OLD BROOKLYN IN EARLY PHOTOGRAPHS, 1865–1929, William Lee Younger. Luna Park, Gravesend race track, construction of Grand Army Plaza, moving of Hotel Brighton, etc. 157 previously unpublished photographs. 165pp. 8⅞ × 11¾. 23587-4 Pa. $13.95

THE MYTHS OF THE NORTH AMERICAN INDIANS, Lewis Spence. Rich anthology of the myths and legends of the Algonquins, Iroquois, Pawnees and Sioux, prefaced by an extensive historical and ethnological commentary. 36 illustrations. 480pp. 5⅜ × 8½. 25967-6 Pa. $8.95

AN ENCYCLOPEDIA OF BATTLES: Accounts of Over 1,560 Battles from 1479 B.C. to the Present, David Eggenberger. Essential details of every major battle in recorded history from the first battle of Megiddo in 1479 B.C. to Grenada in 1984. List of Battle Maps. New Appendix covering the years 1967–1984. Index. 99 illustrations. 544pp. 6½ × 9¼. 24913-1 Pa. $14.95

SAILING ALONE AROUND THE WORLD, Captain Joshua Slocum. First man to sail around the world, alone, in small boat. One of great feats of seamanship told in delightful manner. 67 illustrations. 294pp. 5⅜ × 8½. 20326-3 Pa. $5.95

ANARCHISM AND OTHER ESSAYS, Emma Goldman. Powerful, penetrating, prophetic essays on direct action, role of minorities, prison reform, puritan hypocrisy, violence, etc. 271pp. 5⅜ × 8½. 22484-8 Pa. $5.95

MYTHS OF THE HINDUS AND BUDDHISTS, Ananda K. Coomaraswamy and Sister Nivedita. Great stories of the epics; deeds of Krishna, Shiva, taken from puranas, Vedas, folk tales; etc. 32 illustrations. 400pp. 5⅜ × 8½. 21759-0 Pa. $9.95

BEYOND PSYCHOLOGY, Otto Rank. Fear of death, desire of immortality, nature of sexuality, social organization, creativity, according to Rankian system. 291pp. 5⅜ × 8½. 20485-5 Pa. $8.95

A THEOLOGICO-POLITICAL TREATISE, Benedict Spinoza. Also contains unfinished Political Treatise. Great classic on religious liberty, theory of government on common consent. R. Elwes translation. Total of 421pp. 5⅜ × 8½. 20249-6 Pa. $8.95

MY BONDAGE AND MY FREEDOM, Frederick Douglass. Born a slave, Douglass became outspoken force in antislavery movement. The best of Douglass' autobiographies. Graphic description of slave life. 464pp. 5⅜ × 8½. 22457-0 Pa. $8.95

FOLLOWING THE EQUATOR: A Journey Around the World, Mark Twain. Fascinating humorous account of 1897 voyage to Hawaii, Australia, India, New Zealand, etc. Ironic, bemused reports on peoples, customs, climate, flora and fauna, politics, much more. 197 illustrations. 720pp. 5⅜ × 8½. 26113-1 Pa. $15.95

THE PEOPLE CALLED SHAKERS, Edward D. Andrews. Definitive study of Shakers: origins, beliefs, practices, dances, social organization, furniture and crafts, etc. 33 illustrations. 351pp. 5⅜ × 8½. 21081-2 Pa. $8.95

THE MYTHS OF GREECE AND ROME, H. A. Guerber. A classic of mythology, generously illustrated, long prized for its simple, graphic, accurate retelling of the principal myths of Greece and Rome, and for its commentary on their origins and significance. With 64 illustrations by Michelangelo, Raphael, Titian, Rubens, Canova, Bernini and others. 480pp. 5⅜ × 8½. 27584-1 Pa. $9.95

PSYCHOLOGY OF MUSIC, Carl E. Seashore. Classic work discusses music as a medium from psychological viewpoint. Clear treatment of physical acoustics, auditory apparatus, sound perception, development of musical skills, nature of musical feeling, host of other topics. 88 figures. 408pp. 5⅜ × 8½. 21851-1 Pa. $9.95

THE PHILOSOPHY OF HISTORY, Georg W. Hegel. Great classic of Western thought develops concept that history is not chance but rational process, the evolution of freedom. 457pp. 5⅜ × 8½. 20112-0 Pa. $9.95

THE BOOK OF TEA, Kakuzo Okakura. Minor classic of the Orient: entertaining, charming explanation, interpretation of traditional Japanese culture in terms of tea ceremony. 94pp. 5⅜ × 8½. 20070-1 Pa. $3.95

LIFE IN ANCIENT EGYPT, Adolf Erman. Fullest, most thorough, detailed older account with much not in more recent books, domestic life, religion, magic, medicine, commerce, much more. Many illustrations reproduce tomb paintings, carvings, hieroglyphs, etc. 597pp. 5⅜ × 8½. 22632-8 Pa. $10.95

SUNDIALS, Their Theory and Construction, Albert Waugh. Far and away the best, most thorough coverage of ideas, mathematics concerned, types, construction, adjusting anywhere. Simple, nontechnical treatment allows even children to build several of these dials. Over 100 illustrations. 230pp. 5⅜ × 8½. 22947-5 Pa. $7.95

DYNAMICS OF FLUIDS IN POROUS MEDIA, Jacob Bear. For advanced students of ground water hydrology, soil mechanics and physics, drainage and irrigation engineering, and more. 335 illustrations. Exercises, with answers. 784pp. 6⅛ × 9¼. 65675-6 Pa. $19.95

SONGS OF EXPERIENCE: Facsimile Reproduction with 26 Plates in Full Color, William Blake. 26 full-color plates from a rare 1826 edition. Includes "The Tyger," "London," "Holy Thursday," and other poems. Printed text of poems. 48pp. 5¼ × 7. 24636-1 Pa. $4.95

OLD-TIME VIGNETTES IN FULL COLOR, Carol Belanger Grafton (ed.). Over 390 charming, often sentimental illustrations, selected from archives of Victorian graphics—pretty women posing, children playing, food, flowers, kittens and puppies, smiling cherubs, birds and butterflies, much more. All copyright-free. 48pp. 9¼ × 12¼. 27269-9 Pa. $5.95

PERSPECTIVE FOR ARTISTS, Rex Vicat Cole. Depth, perspective of sky and sea, shadows, much more, not usually covered. 391 diagrams, 81 reproductions of drawings and paintings. 279pp. 5⅜ × 8½. 22487-2 Pa. $6.95

DRAWING THE LIVING FIGURE, Joseph Sheppard. Innovative approach to artistic anatomy focuses on specifics of surface anatomy, rather than muscles and bones. Over 170 drawings of live models in front, back and side views, and in widely varying poses. Accompanying diagrams. 177 illustrations. Introduction. Index. 144pp. 8⅜ × 11¼. 26723-7 Pa. $8.95

GOTHIC AND OLD ENGLISH ALPHABETS: 100 Complete Fonts, Dan X. Solo. Add power, elegance to posters, signs, other graphics with 100 stunning copyright-free alphabets: Blackstone, Dolbey, Germania, 97 more—including many lower-case, numerals, punctuation marks. 104pp. 8⅛ × 11. 24695-7 Pa. $8.95

HOW TO DO BEADWORK, Mary White. Fundamental book on craft from simple projects to five-bead chains and woven works. 106 illustrations. 142pp. 5⅜ × 8. 20697-1 Pa. $4.95

THE BOOK OF WOOD CARVING, Charles Marshall Sayers. Finest book for beginners discusses fundamentals and offers 34 designs. "Absolutely first rate . . . well thought out and well executed."—E. J. Tangerman. 118pp. 7¾ × 10⅝. 23654-4 Pa. $5.95

ILLUSTRATED CATALOG OF CIVIL WAR MILITARY GOODS: Union Army Weapons, Insignia, Uniform Accessories, and Other Equipment, Schuyler, Hartley, and Graham. Rare, profusely illustrated 1846 catalog includes Union Army uniform and dress regulations, arms and ammunition, coats, insignia, flags, swords, rifles, etc. 226 illustrations. 160pp. 9 × 12. 24939-5 Pa. $10.95

WOMEN'S FASHIONS OF THE EARLY 1900s: An Unabridged Republication of "New York Fashions, 1909," National Cloak & Suit Co. Rare catalog of mail-order fashions documents women's and children's clothing styles shortly after the turn of the century. Captions offer full descriptions, prices. Invaluable resource for fashion, costume historians. Approximately 725 illustrations. 128pp. 8⅜ × 11¼. 27276-1 Pa. $11.95

THE 1912 AND 1915 GUSTAV STICKLEY FURNITURE CATALOGS, Gustav Stickley. With over 200 detailed illustrations and descriptions, these two catalogs are essential reading and reference materials and identification guides for Stickley furniture. Captions cite materials, dimensions and prices. 112pp. 6½ × 9¼. 26676-1 Pa. $9.95

EARLY AMERICAN LOCOMOTIVES, John H. White, Jr. Finest locomotive engravings from early 19th century: historical (1804–74), main-line (after 1870), special, foreign, etc. 147 plates. 142pp. 11⅜ × 8¼. 22772-3 Pa. $10.95

THE TALL SHIPS OF TODAY IN PHOTOGRAPHS, Frank O. Braynard. Lavishly illustrated tribute to nearly 100 majestic contemporary sailing vessels: Amerigo Vespucci, Clearwater, Constitution, Eagle, Mayflower, Sea Cloud, Victory, many more. Authoritative captions provide statistics, background on each ship. 190 black-and-white photographs and illustrations. Introduction. 128pp. 8⅞ × 11¾. 27163-3 Pa. $13.95

EARLY NINETEENTH-CENTURY CRAFTS AND TRADES, Peter Stockham (ed.). Extremely rare 1807 volume describes to youngsters the crafts and trades of the day: brickmaker, weaver, dressmaker, bookbinder, ropemaker, saddler, many more. Quaint prose, charming illustrations for each craft. 20 black-and-white line illustrations. 192pp. 4⅜ × 6. 27293-1 Pa. $4.95

VICTORIAN FASHIONS AND COSTUMES FROM HARPER'S BAZAR, 1867–1898, Stella Blum (ed.). Day costumes, evening wear, sports clothes, shoes, hats, other accessories in over 1,000 detailed engravings. 320pp. 9⅜ × 12¼.
22990-4 Pa. $13.95

GUSTAV STICKLEY, THE CRAFTSMAN, Mary Ann Smith. Superb study surveys broad scope of Stickley's achievement, especially in architecture. Design philosophy, rise and fall of the Craftsman empire, descriptions and floor plans for many Craftsman houses, more. 86 black-and-white halftones. 31 line illustrations. Introduction. 208pp. 6½ × 9¼. 27210-9 Pa. $9.95

THE LONG ISLAND RAIL ROAD IN EARLY PHOTOGRAPHS, Ron Ziel. Over 220 rare photos, informative text document origin (1844) and development of rail service on Long Island. Vintage views of early trains, locomotives, stations, passengers, crews, much more. Captions. 8⅞ × 11¾. 26301-0 Pa. $13.95

THE BOOK OF OLD SHIPS: From Egyptian Galleys to Clipper Ships, Henry B. Culver. Superb, authoritative history of sailing vessels, with 80 magnificent line illustrations. Galley, bark, caravel, longship, whaler, many more. Detailed, informative text on each vessel by noted naval historian. Introduction. 256pp. 5⅜ × 8½. 27332-6 Pa. $6.95

TEN BOOKS ON ARCHITECTURE, Vitruvius. The most important book ever written on architecture. Early Roman aesthetics, technology, classical orders, site selection, all other aspects. Morgan translation. 331pp. 5⅜ × 8½. 20645-9 Pa. $8.95

THE HUMAN FIGURE IN MOTION, Eadweard Muybridge. More than 4,500 stopped-action photos, in action series, showing undraped men, women, children jumping, lying down, throwing, sitting, wrestling, carrying, etc. 390pp. 7⅞ × 10⅝.
20204-6 Clothbd. $24.95

TREES OF THE EASTERN AND CENTRAL UNITED STATES AND CANADA, William M. Harlow. Best one-volume guide to 140 trees. Full descriptions, woodlore, range, etc. Over 600 illustrations. Handy size. 288pp. 4½ × 6⅜.
20395-6 Pa. $5.95

SONGS OF WESTERN BIRDS, Dr. Donald J. Borror. Complete song and call repertoire of 60 western species, including flycatchers, juncoes, cactus wrens, many more—includes fully illustrated booklet. Cassette and manual 99913-0 $8.95

GROWING AND USING HERBS AND SPICES, Milo Miloradovich. Versatile handbook provides all the information needed for cultivation and use of all the herbs and spices available in North America. 4 illustrations. Index. Glossary. 236pp. 5⅜ × 8½. 25058-X Pa. $6.95

BIG BOOK OF MAZES AND LABYRINTHS, Walter Shepherd. 50 mazes and labyrinths in all—classical, solid, ripple, and more—in one great volume. Perfect inexpensive puzzler for clever youngsters. Full solutions. 112pp. 8⅛ × 11.
22951-3 Pa. $4.95

PIANO TUNING, J. Cree Fischer. Clearest, best book for beginner, amateur. Simple repairs, raising dropped notes, tuning by easy method of flattened fifths. No previous skills needed. 4 illustrations. 201pp. 5⅜ × 8½. 23267-0 Pa. $5.95

A SOURCE BOOK IN THEATRICAL HISTORY, A. M. Nagler. Contemporary observers on acting, directing, make-up, costuming, stage props, machinery, scene design, from Ancient Greece to Chekhov. 611pp. 5⅜ × 8½. 20515-0 Pa. $11.95

THE COMPLETE NONSENSE OF EDWARD LEAR, Edward Lear. All nonsense limericks, zany alphabets, Owl and Pussycat, songs, nonsense botany, etc., illustrated by Lear. Total of 320pp. 5⅜ × 8½. (USO) 20167-8 Pa. $6.95

VICTORIAN PARLOUR POETRY: An Annotated Anthology, Michael R. Turner. 117 gems by Longfellow, Tennyson, Browning, many lesser-known poets. "The Village Blacksmith," "Curfew Must Not Ring Tonight," "Only a Baby Small," dozens more, often difficult to find elsewhere. Index of poets, titles, first lines. xxiii + 325pp. 5⅜ × 8¼. 27044-0 Pa. $8.95

DUBLINERS, James Joyce. Fifteen stories offer vivid, tightly focused observations of the lives of Dublin's poorer classes. At least one, "The Dead," is considered a masterpiece. Reprinted complete and unabridged from standard edition. 160pp. 5³⁄₁₆ × 8¼. 26870-5 Pa. $1.00

THE HAUNTED MONASTERY and THE CHINESE MAZE MURDERS, Robert van Gulik. Two full novels by van Gulik, set in 7th-century China, continue adventures of Judge Dee and his companions. An evil Taoist monastery, seemingly supernatural events; overgrown topiary maze hides strange crimes. 27 illustrations. 328pp. 5⅜ × 8½. 23502-5 Pa. $7.95

THE BOOK OF THE SACRED MAGIC OF ABRAMELIN THE MAGE, translated by S. MacGregor Mathers. Medieval manuscript of ceremonial magic. Basic document in Aleister Crowley, Golden Dawn groups. 268pp. 5⅜ × 8½. 23211-5 Pa. $8.95

NEW RUSSIAN-ENGLISH AND ENGLISH-RUSSIAN DICTIONARY, M. A. O'Brien. This is a remarkably handy Russian dictionary, containing a surprising amount of information, including over 70,000 entries. 366pp. 4½ × 6⅛. 20208-9 Pa. $9.95

HISTORIC HOMES OF THE AMERICAN PRESIDENTS, Second, Revised Edition, Irvin Haas. A traveler's guide to American Presidential homes, most open to the public, depicting and describing homes occupied by every American President from George Washington to George Bush. With visiting hours, admission charges, travel routes. 175 photographs. Index. 160pp. 8¼ × 11. 26751-2 Pa. $10.95

NEW YORK IN THE FORTIES, Andreas Feininger. 162 brilliant photographs by the well-known photographer, formerly with *Life* magazine. Commuters, shoppers, Times Square at night, much else from city at its peak. Captions by John von Hartz. 181pp. 9¼ × 10¾. 23585-8 Pa. $12.95

INDIAN SIGN LANGUAGE, William Tomkins. Over 525 signs developed by Sioux and other tribes. Written instructions and diagrams. Also 290 pictographs. 111pp. 6⅛ × 9¼. 22029-X Pa. $3.50

ANATOMY: A Complete Guide for Artists, Joseph Sheppard. A master of figure drawing shows artists how to render human anatomy convincingly. Over 460 illustrations. 224pp. 8⅜ × 11¼. 27279-6 Pa. $10.95

MEDIEVAL CALLIGRAPHY: Its History and Technique, Marc Drogin. Spirited history, comprehensive instruction manual covers 13 styles (ca. 4th century thru 15th). Excellent photographs; directions for duplicating medieval techniques with modern tools. 224pp. 8⅜ × 11¼. 26142-5 Pa. $11.95

DRIED FLOWERS: How to Prepare Them, Sarah Whitlock and Martha Rankin. Complete instructions on how to use silica gel, meal and borax, perlite aggregate, sand and borax, glycerine and water to create attractive permanent flower arrangements. 12 illustrations. 32pp. 5⅜ × 8½. 21802-3 Pa. $1.00

EASY-TO-MAKE BIRD FEEDERS FOR WOODWORKERS, Scott D. Campbell. Detailed, simple-to-use guide for designing, constructing, caring for and using feeders. Text, illustrations for 12 classic and contemporary designs. 96pp. 5⅜ × 8½. 25847-5 Pa. $2.95

OLD-TIME CRAFTS AND TRADES, Peter Stockham. An 1807 book created to teach children about crafts and trades open to them as future careers. It describes in detailed, nontechnical terms 24 different occupations, among them coachmaker, gardener, hairdresser, lacemaker, shoemaker, wheelwright, copper-plate printer, milliner, trunkmaker, merchant and brewer. Finely detailed engravings illustrate each occupation. 192pp. 4⅝ × 6. 27398-9 Pa. $4.95

THE HISTORY OF UNDERCLOTHES, C. Willett Cunnington and Phyllis Cunnington. Fascinating, well-documented survey covering six centuries of English undergarments, enhanced with over 100 illustrations: 12th-century laced-up bodice, footed long drawers (1795), 19th-century bustles, 19th-century corsets for men, Victorian "bust improvers," much more. 272pp. 5⅜ × 8¼. 27124-2 Pa. $9.95

ARTS AND CRAFTS FURNITURE: The Complete Brooks Catalog of 1912, Brooks Manufacturing Co. Photos and detailed descriptions of more than 150 now very collectible furniture designs from the Arts and Crafts movement depict davenports, settees, buffets, desks, tables, chairs, bedsteads, dressers and more, all built of solid, quarter-sawed oak. Invaluable for students and enthusiasts of antiques, Americana and the decorative arts. 80pp. 6½ × 9¼. 27471-3 Pa. $7.95

HOW WE INVENTED THE AIRPLANE: An Illustrated History, Orville Wright. Fascinating firsthand account covers early experiments, construction of planes and motors, first flights, much more. Introduction and commentary by Fred C. Kelly. 76 photographs. 96pp. 8¼ × 11. 25662-6 Pa. $8.95

THE ARTS OF THE SAILOR: Knotting, Splicing and Ropework, Hervey Garrett Smith. Indispensable shipboard reference covers tools, basic knots and useful hitches; handsewing and canvas work, more. Over 100 illustrations. Delightful reading for sea lovers. 256pp. 5⅜ × 8½. 26440-8 Pa. $7.95

FRANK LLOYD WRIGHT'S FALLINGWATER: The House and Its History, Second, Revised Edition, Donald Hoffmann. A total revision—both in text and illustrations—of the standard document on Fallingwater, the boldest, most personal architectural statement of Wright's mature years, updated with valuable new material from the recently opened Frank Lloyd Wright Archives. "Fascinating"—*The New York Times*. 116 illustrations. 128pp. 9¼ × 10¾. 27430-6 Pa. $10.95

PHOTOGRAPHIC SKETCHBOOK OF THE CIVIL WAR, Alexander Gardner. 100 photos taken on field during the Civil War. Famous shots of Manassas, Harper's Ferry, Lincoln, Richmond, slave pens, etc. 244pp. 10⅝ × 8¼.
22731-6 Pa. $9.95

FIVE ACRES AND INDEPENDENCE, Maurice G. Kains. Great back-to-the-land classic explains basics of self-sufficient farming. The one book to get. 95 illustrations. 397pp. 5⅜ × 8½.
20974-1 Pa. $7.95

SONGS OF EASTERN BIRDS, Dr. Donald J. Borror. Songs and calls of 60 species most common to eastern U.S.: warblers, woodpeckers, flycatchers, thrushes, larks, many more in high-quality recording.
Cassette and manual 99912-2 $8.95

A MODERN HERBAL, Margaret Grieve. Much the fullest, most exact, most useful compilation of herbal material. Gigantic alphabetical encyclopedia, from aconite to zedoary, gives botanical information, medical properties, folklore, economic uses, much else. Indispensable to serious reader. 161 illustrations. 888pp. 6½ × 9¼. 2-vol. set. (USO)
Vol. I: 22798-7 Pa. $9.95
Vol. II: 22799-5 Pa. $9.95

HIDDEN TREASURE MAZE BOOK, Dave Phillips. Solve 34 challenging mazes accompanied by heroic tales of adventure. Evil dragons, people-eating plants, bloodthirsty giants, many more dangerous adversaries lurk at every twist and turn. 34 mazes, stories, solutions. 48pp. 8¼ × 11.
24566-7 Pa. $2.95

LETTERS OF W. A. MOZART, Wolfgang A. Mozart. Remarkable letters show bawdy wit, humor, imagination, musical insights, contemporary musical world; includes some letters from Leopold Mozart. 276pp. 5⅜ × 8½.
22859-2 Pa. $7.95

BASIC PRINCIPLES OF CLASSICAL BALLET, Agrippina Vaganova. Great Russian theoretician, teacher explains methods for teaching classical ballet. 118 illustrations. 175pp. 5⅜ × 8½.
22036-2 Pa. $4.95

THE JUMPING FROG, Mark Twain. Revenge edition. The original story of The Celebrated Jumping Frog of Calaveras County, a hapless French translation, and Twain's hilarious "retranslation" from the French. 12 illustrations. 66pp. 5⅜ × 8½.
22686-7 Pa. $3.95

BEST REMEMBERED POEMS, Martin Gardner (ed.). The 126 poems in this superb collection of 19th- and 20th-century British and American verse range from Shelley's "To a Skylark" to the impassioned "Renascence" of Edna St. Vincent Millay and to Edward Lear's whimsical "The Owl and the Pussycat." 224pp. 5⅜ × 8½.
27165-X Pa. $4.95

COMPLETE SONNETS, William Shakespeare. Over 150 exquisite poems deal with love, friendship, the tyranny of time, beauty's evanescence, death and other themes in language of remarkable power, precision and beauty. Glossary of archaic terms. 80pp. 5³⁄₁₆ × 8¼.
26686-9 Pa. $1.00

BODIES IN A BOOKSHOP, R. T. Campbell. Challenging mystery of blackmail and murder with ingenious plot and superbly drawn characters. In the best tradition of British suspense fiction. 192pp. 5⅜ × 8½.
24720-1 Pa. $5.95

THE WIT AND HUMOR OF OSCAR WILDE, Alvin Redman (ed.). More than 1,000 ripostes, paradoxes, wisecracks: Work is the curse of the drinking classes; I can resist everything except temptation; etc. 258pp. 5⅜ × 8½. **20602-5 Pa. $5.95**

SHAKESPEARE LEXICON AND QUOTATION DICTIONARY, Alexander Schmidt. Full definitions, locations, shades of meaning in every word in plays and poems. More than 50,000 exact quotations. 1,485pp. 6½ × 9¼. 2-vol. set.
Vol. I: **22726-X Pa. $16.95**
Vol. 2: **22727-8 Pa. $15.95**

SELECTED POEMS, Emily Dickinson. Over 100 best-known, best-loved poems by one of America's foremost poets, reprinted from authoritative early editions. No comparable edition at this price. Index of first lines. 64pp. 5 3/16 × 8¼.
26466-1 Pa. $1.00

CELEBRATED CASES OF JUDGE DEE (DEE GOONG AN), translated by Robert van Gulik. Authentic 18th-century Chinese detective novel; Dee and associates solve three interlocked cases. Led to van Gulik's own stories with same characters. Extensive introduction. 9 illustrations. 237pp. 5⅜ × 8½.
23337-5 Pa. $6.95

THE MALLEUS MALEFICARUM OF KRAMER AND SPRENGER, translated by Montague Summers. Full text of most important witchhunter's "bible," used by both Catholics and Protestants. 278pp. 6⅝ × 10. **22802-9 Pa. $11.95**

SPANISH STORIES/CUENTOS ESPAÑOLES: A Dual-Language Book, Angel Flores (ed.). Unique format offers 13 great stories in Spanish by Cervantes, Borges, others. Faithful English translations on facing pages. 352pp. 5⅜ × 8½.
25399-6 Pa. $8.95

THE CHICAGO WORLD'S FAIR OF 1893: A Photographic Record, Stanley Appelbaum (ed.). 128 rare photos show 200 buildings, Beaux-Arts architecture, Midway, original Ferris Wheel, Edison's kinetoscope, more. Architectural emphasis; full text. 116pp. 8¼ × 11. **23990-X Pa. $9.95**

OLD QUEENS, N.Y., IN EARLY PHOTOGRAPHS, Vincent F. Seyfried and William Asadorian. Over 160 rare photographs of Maspeth, Jamaica, Jackson Heights, and other areas. Vintage views of DeWitt Clinton mansion, 1939 World's Fair and more. Captions. 192pp. 8⅞ × 11. **26358-4 Pa. $12.95**

CAPTURED BY THE INDIANS: 15 Firsthand Accounts, 1750–1870, Frederick Drimmer. Astounding true historical accounts of grisly torture, bloody conflicts, relentless pursuits, miraculous escapes and more, by people who lived to tell the tale. 384pp. 5⅜ × 8½. **24901-8 Pa. $8.95**

THE WORLD'S GREAT SPEECHES, Lewis Copeland and Lawrence W. Lamm (eds.). Vast collection of 278 speeches of Greeks to 1970. Powerful and effective models; unique look at history. 842pp. 5⅜ × 8½. **20468-5 Pa. $14.95**

THE BOOK OF THE SWORD, Sir Richard F. Burton. Great Victorian scholar/adventurer's eloquent, erudite history of the "queen of weapons"—from prehistory to early Roman Empire. Evolution and development of early swords, variations (sabre, broadsword, cutlass, scimitar, etc.), much more. 336pp. 6⅛ × 9¼. **25434-8 Pa. $8.95**

AUTOBIOGRAPHY: The Story of My Experiments with Truth, Mohandas K. Gandhi. Boyhood, legal studies, purification, the growth of the Satyagraha (nonviolent protest) movement. Critical, inspiring work of the man responsible for the freedom of India. 480pp. 5⅜ × 8½. (USO)　24593-4 Pa. $8.95

CELTIC MYTHS AND LEGENDS, T. W. Rolleston. Masterful retelling of Irish and Welsh stories and tales. Cuchulain, King Arthur, Deirdre, the Grail, many more. First paperback edition. 58 full-page illustrations. 512pp. 5⅜ × 8½.
26507-2 Pa. $9.95

THE PRINCIPLES OF PSYCHOLOGY, William James. Famous long course complete, unabridged. Stream of thought, time perception, memory, experimental methods; great work decades ahead of its time. 94 figures. 1,391pp. 5⅜×8½. 2-vol. set.
Vol. I: 20381-6 Pa. $12.95
Vol. II: 20382-4 Pa. $12.95

THE WORLD AS WILL AND REPRESENTATION, Arthur Schopenhauer. Definitive English translation of Schopenhauer's life work, correcting more than 1,000 errors, omissions in earlier translations. Translated by E. F. J. Payne. Total of 1,269pp. 5⅜ × 8½. 2-vol. set.
Vol. 1: 21761-2 Pa. $11.95
Vol. 2: 21762-0 Pa. $11.95

MAGIC AND MYSTERY IN TIBET, Madame Alexandra David-Neel. Experiences among lamas, magicians, sages, sorcerers, Bonpa wizards. A true psychic discovery. 32 illustrations. 321pp. 5⅜ × 8½. (USO)　22682-4 Pa. $8.95

THE EGYPTIAN BOOK OF THE DEAD, E. A. Wallis Budge. Complete reproduction of Ani's papyrus, finest ever found. Full hieroglyphic text, interlinear transliteration, word-for-word translation, smooth translation. 533pp. 6½ × 9¼.
21866-X Pa. $9.95

MATHEMATICS FOR THE NONMATHEMATICIAN, Morris Kline. Detailed, college-level treatment of mathematics in cultural and historical context, with numerous exercises. Recommended Reading Lists. Tables. Numerous figures. 641pp. 5⅜ × 8½.　24823-2 Pa. $11.95

THEORY OF WING SECTIONS: Including a Summary of Airfoil Data, Ira H. Abbott and A. E. von Doenhoff. Concise compilation of subsonic aerodynamic characteristics of NACA wing sections, plus description of theory. 350pp. of tables. 693pp. 5⅜ × 8½.　60586-8 Pa. $14.95

THE RIME OF THE ANCIENT MARINER, Gustave Doré, S. T. Coleridge. Doré's finest work; 34 plates capture moods, subtleties of poem. Flawless full-size reproductions printed on facing pages with authoritative text of poem. "Beautiful. Simply beautiful."—*Publisher's Weekly.* 77pp. 9¼ × 12.　22305-1 Pa. $6.95

NORTH AMERICAN INDIAN DESIGNS FOR ARTISTS AND CRAFTS-PEOPLE, Eva Wilson. Over 360 authentic copyright-free designs adapted from Navajo blankets, Hopi pottery, Sioux buffalo hides, more. Geometrics, symbolic figures, plant and animal motifs, etc. 128pp. 8⅜ × 11. (EUK)　25341-4 Pa. $7.95

SCULPTURE: Principles and Practice, Louis Slobodkin. Step-by-step approach to clay, plaster, metals, stone; classical and modern. 253 drawings, photos. 255pp. 8⅛ × 11.　22960-2 Pa. $10.95

THE INFLUENCE OF SEA POWER UPON HISTORY, 1660–1783, A. T. Mahan. Influential classic of naval history and tactics still used as text in war colleges. First paperback edition. 4 maps. 24 battle plans. 640pp. 5⅜ × 8½.
25509-3 Pa. $12.95

THE STORY OF THE TITANIC AS TOLD BY ITS SURVIVORS, Jack Winocour (ed.). What it was really like. Panic, despair, shocking inefficiency, and a little heroism. More thrilling than any fictional account. 26 illustrations. 320pp. 5⅜ × 8½. **20610-6 Pa. $8.95**

FAIRY AND FOLK TALES OF THE IRISH PEASANTRY, William Butler Yeats (ed.). Treasury of 64 tales from the twilight world of Celtic myth and legend: "The Soul Cages," "The Kildare Pooka," "King O'Toole and his Goose," many more. Introduction and Notes by W. B. Yeats. 352pp. 5⅜ × 8½. **26941-8 Pa. $8.95**

BUDDHIST MAHAYANA TEXTS, E. B. Cowell and Others (eds.). Superb, accurate translations of basic documents in Mahayana Buddhism, highly important in history of religions. The Buddha-karita of Asvaghosha, Larger Sukhavativyuha, more. 448pp. 5⅜ × 8½. 25552-2 Pa. $9.95

ONE TWO THREE . . . INFINITY: Facts and Speculations of Science, George Gamow. Great physicist's fascinating, readable overview of contemporary science: number theory, relativity, fourth dimension, entropy, genes, atomic structure, much more. 128 illustrations. Index. 352pp. 5⅜ × 8½. **25664-2 Pa. $8.95**

ENGINEERING IN HISTORY, Richard Shelton Kirby, et al. Broad, nontechnical survey of history's major technological advances: birth of Greek science, industrial revolution, electricity and applied science, 20th-century automation, much more. 181 illustrations. ". . . excellent . . ."—Isis. Bibliography. vii + 530pp. 5⅜ × 8¼.
26412-2 Pa. $14.95

Prices subject to change without notice.

Available at your book dealer or write for free catalog to Dept. GI, Dover Publications, Inc., 31 East 2nd St., Mineola, N.Y. 11501. Dover publishes more than 500 books each year on science, elementary and advanced mathematics, biology, music, art, literary history, social sciences and other areas.